THE ULTIMATE FEAST

30-days of spiritual meals,
feasting on Jesus and His Word

PAULA LUTZE

Book Cover by Christian Rafetto

First edition 2024

Come sit at the Lord's table and feast on all He has for you.

How happy are those who will sit down at the feast in the Kingdom of God!

Luke 14:15b (GNT)

He placed me at his banquet table, for everyone to see that his banner over me declares his love.

Song of Songs 2:4 (VOICE)

People will come from the east and the west, from the north and the south, and sit down at the feast in the Kingdom of God.

Luke 13:29 (GNT)

DEDICATION

I dedicate this book to my husband, James. You are my best friend, favorite food critic, wonderful father, and inspiration to walk in the Lord without measure. You have taught me so much as we have feasted on the Lord together. I love you.

TOASTS

To my Beloved Savior. You pull my chair out for me at your table every day. To dine with you is to truly live a life that surpasses my greatest imagination. To you, I raise the Communion Cup. I will always remember what you finished on the cross and celebrate with joy. Shalom!

To my two beautiful daughters, Elaina and Ellie. I am so grateful for how you teach me what the love of Jesus looks like. You are walking testaments to God's glory and miracles. To you, I raise my cup filled with momma pride and great expectation. Cheers!

To my parents, Rick and Sue. You raised me up in the ways of the Lord and taught me that anything is possible in Christ. Your lives have always been an inspiration to me. I'm so grateful you taught me to find truth in the Word and not based on someone else's words. To you, I raise my glass filled with admiration and gratefulness. Sláinte and Prost!

To the world changers, Georgian and Winnie Cóco Banov. The message that you two carry changed my life forever. You have taught me so much about Christ and union with Him. God used you to help me encounter His joy, and now I get to share it with others! To you, I raise a mug filled with hot coco. Saluti!

To my spiritual sister, Sara Beeler. You are a mighty woman of God. When you pray, you shift the atmosphere for the kingdom of heaven. When I was lost, you prayed me home. I'm so proud of how you showcase the love of Jesus with your life. To you, I raise a coffee cup filled with His special brew as we change the world one person at a time. Kanpai!

To my extended family, Chris, Angela, Ashton, and Savannah. You are always so generous and have a way of reflecting Jesus like no others I know. You still inspire me to be more like Jesus. To you, I raise my soda can filled to overflowing with a heart of love. Cheers!

T H E   M E N U

Toasts	....	7
Foreword	Taste-Tester Testimonial................................	11
Wine List	....	15
Appetizer	....	17
DAY 1	Feast on His Love	21
DAY 2	Feast on His Finished Work	27
DAY 3	Feast on His Joy.....................................	33
DAY 4	Feast on His Faith...................................	39
DAY 5	Feast on His Healing	45
DAY 6	Feast on His Word	55
DAY 7	Feast on His Grace	63
DAY 8	Feast on His Presence................................	69
DAY 9	Feast on His Intimacy	75
DAY 10	Feast on His Righteousness	81
DAY 11	Feast on His Spirit	87
DAY 12	Feast on His Bread	103
DAY 13	Feast on His Wine....................................	109
DAY 14	Feast on His Promises	117
DAY 15	Feast on His Victory.................................	123
DAY 16	Feast on His Goodness...............................	131

DAY 17   Feast on His Forgiveness 139

DAY 18   Feast on His Glory 145

DAY 19   Feast on His Holiness 151

DAY 20   Feast on His Freedom 159

DAY 21   Feast on His Perspective 165

DAY 22   Feast on His Bliss 171

DAY 23   Feast on His Prayer 177

DAY 24   Feast on His Compassion............................... 185

DAY 25   Feast on His Wisdom 193

DAY 26   Feast on His Kingdom 201

DAY 27   Feast on His Authority................................ 209

DAY 28   Feast on His Abundance 215

DAY 29   Feast on His Name.................................... 221

DAY 30   Feast on His Fullness................................. 227

RESOURCES   233

FOREWORD

TASTE-TESTER TESTIMONIAL

Paula Lutze is a "chef de jour," serving us a Royal Banquet. She has made the Word of God an edible, delectable feast: sweet, savory, and spicy, sure to become your daily food and drink. She knows how to take a heavenly recipe, explain the ingredients, put them all together, and serve you an unforgettable meal. She is not just talking about it; she is sampling the goods and experiencing on a daily basis how to eat the Lamb of God and drink His outpoured love wine. She has collected these recipes from multiple cookbooks (translations) and is generously sharing them with us. Enter the banquet hall through the door of the crucified Christ and take your seat, co-seated with the Bridegroom. Delight yourself in the wine list, appetizers, main course—and of course, we won't forget the desserts! You will be guided through the nutrition labels to make sure the spiritual food you are consuming is pure, organic, and fresh, guaranteed to keep you holy and happy all the days of your life on this earth.

Highlighting some of the basics on the menu, let's talk about Bread and Wine. Jesus offers us His body and blood, promising to abide, dwell, and remain in us and with us (John 6). Jesus is the true bread of heaven, the Bread of Life, who gave Himself to the world. Anyone eating this living bread will live forever. The bread Jesus gives us is His flesh: He did this on the cross, giving Himself to us as the Crucified One. Jesus said that without eating this feast, the Flesh and Blood of the Son of Man, you have no life in you. "He who feeds on My flesh and drinks My blood dwells continually in Me, and I [in like manner dwell continually] in him" (John 6:56, AMPC).

We learn about the wine garden from Song of Solomon, the greatest song King Solomon ever wrote. There we find the banquet table and the wine hall. Let the Holy Spirit take us there and teach us how to drink the love wine with our beloved Bridegroom. The Trinity desires that we live intoxicated with love at this banquet feast. Every believer is destined to realize union with the Bridegroom, and so a question arises: can we fast while the Bridegroom is with us? This is not the time for fasting. This feast is costly and rare; all has been provided, all is ready as the Father has declared, and you have a seat at His table reserved exclusively for you.

We will learn to feast on intimacy with Christ the Bridegroom as He invites you to be co-crucified with Him in the closest possible union, co-buried, co-raised, and co-seated at His table. Paul tells us in 1 Corinthians 10:4 that all of Israel ate the same spiritual food and drank the same spiritual drink. That drink was Christ. From the Old Covenant recipe book, nourishing manna that fell in the wilderness was a type of Christ and was called the food of angels. Now the church has been given a new diet. When Christ was incarnate, He ate food with men, desiring to give Himself—His body, His flesh—for us on the cross. His blood poured out is the New Wine, the "Spirit given without measure," and is still flowing today for all who are thirsty. One drink of the living water will turn into endless, effervescent, flowing rivers of love wine for others. Oh, the bliss of those who drink this intoxicating love wine!

You will also learn that you are already feasting on His righteousness. When we believe in the One that raised Christ from the dead, we are reckoned or accounted by God as being righteous. Now in right standing with God we can have sweet communion with our Lord the Bridegroom, the gracious Father, and the overwhelming Holy Spirit. Music and dancing are part of every meal. We have been invited into the dance of the Holy Trinity, where they are singing and rejoicing over us (Zephaniah 3:17).

As you eat this foundational meal of the Crucified Lamb, you are entering into His finished work of the cross. Anointed with the spiced oil of joy for His death, Jesus was prepared from the foundation of the world. His blood was given, not taken, and has turned into the rarest and most ancient vintage of "love wine" the universe has ever known. Let Him bring you to His wine cellar to feast on His crucified body until you faint in His presence, falling down as a dead man like John in Revelation 1:17 or the Queen of Sheba fainting as she beheld Solomon's kingdom exclaiming not even half had been told her (1 Kings 10:1-13).

Ahhhhhhh....finally the desserts! Raise your glass of "power punch" in a glory toast as you sample "bliss-filled treats," the "Bridegroom's cake," and finally the "wedding cake" experiencing firsthand that the desserts are truly heavenly, from another realm. Eat all you like to help you gain some glory weight, the heavy *kabod* (glory) of God. Notice how prayers of thanksgiving arise continually from your heart before, during, and after every bite.

My recommendation for this "seven star" Ultimate Feast is to eat it all, if you are able, sampling and tasting everything that your Bridegroom offers. And by the way, the bill has already been taken care of (no tips allowed)! *Bon appetite!*

**Please leave a review if you have enjoyed this restaurant.

Winnie Cóco Banov
Co-founder of Global Celebration and GCSSM
(Global Celebration School of Supernatural Ministry)
Author of *Love Notes: The Essential Guide to Your Marriage Union with Christ*, *The Proposal*, and more

WINE LIST

NEW WINE

For our beverage selection we only have one option: New Wine. As a frequent drinker of this Wine, I must say it is the best beverage you will ever taste.

The Spirit of Jesus is our New Wine. The more we drink Him in, the more we experience a new way of thinking and living. His Spirit is the Holy Spirit. Jesus tells us to come to Him and drink (John 7:37). His Spirit empowers us to live a life that breaks through the natural realm and into the spirit realm. The more we drink this New Wine, the more rivers of living water spring forth.

New Wine Description: The New Wine is a complex wine filled with rich, opulent flavors, aromas, and elegance. Some of these aromas include notes of love, joy, patience, and all other fruits of the Spirit. The New Wine is a full-bodied, perfectly balanced (in a triune) wine that includes the complex flavors of the Blood, the Lion, and a hint of the Lamb. This Wine has a long finish which, once tasted, lingers on the palate for all eternity.

NEW WINE
TASTING TIPS

- *See:* Observe the beauty and the clarity of the *substance* of the Wine. The substance of this Wine is comprised of the *Father*, the *Son*, and the *Holy Spirit*. The more you drink, the more you will see all three.
- *Swirl:* Swirling brings out the properties of the Wine. This increases the Wine's *contact* and *intensifies its aroma*. This Wine will flow inside and all around you, filling you with all the *notes of the Spirit*.
- *Smell:* Smell the *fragrance* of the Wine. Let the *aroma of heaven* fill you up.
- *Sip:* The first sip will allow you to sample the *whole body* of the Wine. You will be able to taste the *Father's love, the Son's intimacy, and the Spirit's power*.
- *Savor:* Drinking the New Wine is an *experience*. Each sip is supposed to be *absorbed* into your body. Each sip causes you to become more susceptible to the *intoxication of Jesus*.

Warning: Once tasted, this Wine can cause extreme joy, uncontrollable laughter, the inability to stand/walk straight, and healing in the body, mind, and heart.

APPETIZER

The meals prepared for you over the next 30 days will change your life. These meals are supernatural in nature. They have the potential to alter all areas of your life, including areas that seem unchangeable at the present. When we eat, food metabolizes and gives our body nutrients. These nutrients benefit not only our bodies but also our minds and emotions. Feasting on Jesus is the same. Each portion of Him that we consume goes inside us, is absorbed, and gives our entire being His living sustenance.

God doesn't just want to be *with* us but dwell *in* us and flow *out* of us. The Lord wants to be intimately connected to us. He wants to bless our lives so much that everywhere we go, people see His favor all over us and His nature spilling out of us. He wants us to devour all that He is so that we can live out heaven on earth, here and now. If you consume Him, He will be closer to you than ever. To get the most out of these meals, I want you to sit at His table every day.

These meals also have a special bonus feature. They are the only meals where the more you eat, the less you will weigh. I know it sounds too good to be true, but it is. When you feast during these 30 days, you will see the weight of guilt, shame, failure, broken relationships, regret, and many more burdens come off. The more you dine on Jesus, the lighter you will feel, guaranteed!

There is no fast food here. We don't want to take something into ourselves that is of less quality than our True Food. Jesus called Himself

"True Food," the words of life in the flesh. If you like comfort food, these meals are packed full! If you like spicy food, you are at the right table. If you like organic food, this is the purest True Food you will ever eat. I'll start you off with these 30 days so you can become accustomed to dining on the Lord, but the ultimate feast is endless. My hope is that you will use all the flavors of heaven—all the spices of the Holy Spirit—and create your own meals with the Lamb. Sit and feast at His table every day.

Spiritual Meal Plans

I created this book to resemble a meal plan guide to help others see the importance of getting our daily portion of the Bread of Life. My inspiration came when I read, "give us our daily bread" in the Lord's Model Prayer. What if Jesus, who called Himself the Bread of Life, was teaching His disciples to pray for more than merely physical bread? I realized that I can rely on Him for more than physical nourishment. He is also the One who provides all my spiritual nutrition.

1 Corinthians 5:8 says, "So let us feast upon him and grow strong in the Christian life, leaving entirely behind us the cancerous old life with all its hatreds and wickedness. Let us feast instead upon the pure bread of honor and sincerity and truth" (TLB). The Word tells us to feast on Him. This means that we need to get into the kitchen and marinate with the Lamb! Once I started to speak of intimacy with Jesus using cooking and feasting terms, people started to react differently. They saw how food consumption relates to spending time with Jesus, thinking about Jesus, and then absorbing Jesus. God is so creative, and He gives us His creativity. I hope that you enjoy sitting at His table, not just observing the ultimate feast but eating as much as you can.

Meal Layout

Food for Thought: At the top of every meal, you will see a Food for Thought. This is where I have included some questions or statements to chew on while we feast. They are designed to help you meditate on things from a different perspective.

Main Course: The main course is the meal itself. This is where you will spend time at the Lord's table, savoring all that He is as we feast on different portions of the whole Lamb.

Nutrition Labels: I have included nutrition labels after every meal so you can see what happens when you consume each specific day's meal. These labels are also supposed to bring a smile to your face and empowerment to your spirit.

Dessert: After every nutrition label, there will be dessert. Desserts are specifically prepared to activate you in different ways. These desserts will push you to step out of your comfort zone and reflect on how you think and feel about the application of God's Word in your life. Some of the Reflection Questions in the dessert might take some time to answer. Please do not rush. Take time throughout each day and reflect. These questions are designed to make you think about the Lord and yourself in ways you haven't before. These desserts are meant to be enjoyed with the Holy Spirit and sometimes your friends!

Setting: These meals are designed to be eaten at the Lord's table. Take time every day to find a place without distraction and enjoy each bite. Savor all the exquisite flavors and spices of all He is. I recommend that you go back and retry your favorite meals as often as you can. Remember, a table is a place to sit, eat, and enjoy.

> *"So, whether you eat or drink, or whatever you do, do all to the glory of God." (1 Corinthians 10:31, ESV)*

In this book we will eat and drink to glorify God! *Bon appetite!*

DAY 1

FEAST ON HIS LOVE

> **Food for Thought:** Food is meant for consumption. Jesus says He is true food.

For I am convinced that nothing can ever separate us from his love. Death can't, and life can't. The angels won't, and all the powers of hell itself cannot keep God's love away. Our fears for today, our worries about tomorrow, or where we are—high above the sky, or in the deepest ocean—nothing will ever be able to separate us from the love of God demonstrated by our Lord Jesus Christ when he died for us.

Romans 8:38-39 (TLB)

What is Love?

I grew up hearing an Austrian Proverb that says, "Love nourishes the soul like food nourishes the body." I would say that love doesn't just nourish the soul but everything within us because Jesus *is* love. Love. This word is so powerful. This one little word changes everything when we truly grasp what it means in Christ. Love takes us from being identified as orphans to being set up as sons and daughters. Love is Jesus picking you up wherever you are, embracing you, and sitting you down at His table. He wants us to feast on His love because the more we feast, the more love we intake, and the more love we can pour out.

In John 15:9 Jesus tells us to abide in His love or as the Message says, "Make yourselves at home in my love." I want you to stop for a moment and just think about that. Make your home in His love. Imagine His love is where you live. It is where you start your day and lay your head down at night. His love can be your dwelling place. His love casts out fear (1 John 4:18). This can be a fear of punishment, fear of man, fear of imperfection—anything. His love is always stronger. His love is always victorious. Rest in His love today.

His Love for Us

Jesus loves us so much that He went to the cross for us, so that we might know Him and dwell with Him (John 3:16). His love is the beginning of everything. I am convinced that Jesus' love is the foundational ingredient for a well-balanced, nutritious life. If we do not understand His love for us, how can we expect to pass love on to others?

Jesus doesn't look at you and see someone who is dirty, unworthy, or unlovable. It doesn't matter what you have done throughout your life or the mistakes you have made. He knew you when He went to the cross. He saw you all those years ago when He hung there taking His final breaths. He loved you and thought of you when He gave up His life. You are the most valuable thing in existence to Him. He wants you to experience His love right now. His love is not withheld from you until you "get yourself right" or until you get to heaven. It is already prepared and available at His table, ready for you to feast. I've also got good news for you: it is an endless supply!

One of my favorite visuals of love in the Bible is when Jesus is teaching in the temple, and the religious leaders bring a woman caught in adultery to the center of the temple court (John 8:1-11). I can see this woman being dragged in, maybe even not fully clothed since she was caught in the act. She is right in the middle, where everyone can see her, and she is surrounded by accusing voices. The religious leaders state to Jesus how the law demands that she be killed for her actions. What does Jesus do? He stoops down and writes a message on the ground with His finger. The Bible doesn't tell us what He writes, but I have a feeling it is some form of message about love. John 3:17 in the Message says, "God didn't go to all the trouble of sending his Son *merely to point an accusing finger*, telling the world how bad it was. He came to help, to put the world right again. *Anyone who trusts in him is acquitted*" (italics added for emphasis).

This woman is standing there, hearing all these accusing voices and seeing all those fingers pointed at her. Jesus has every right to accuse her. He has every right to punish her. However, He straightens up and says, "Let anyone of you without sin cast the first stone." One by one, the accusing voices depart, and once they are all gone, Jesus looks at the woman. He asks if anyone else is around and then tells her that He does not condemn her either. He goes one step further and tells her to sin no more.

Jesus loved this woman. He loved her even when she was caught in the act. He acquitted her from punishment. I imagine myself as that woman, caught up in my mistakes, hearing people around me talking about my faults and bringing up my past. But then comes Jesus. He stoops down and writes a love letter to me, explaining how much He values me and how the past doesn't represent the present. I then realize that all my mistakes disappear in His love and forgiveness; all of them, never to be remembered. His love breaks through everything that you thought you ruined, including yourself, and makes it new!

I pray that you may experience His love. To experience something means to participate in it. Then you can truly understand why Paul wrote about experiencing God's love in his letter to the church in Ephesus.

> May He grant you out of the riches of His glory, to be strength-
> ened and spiritually energized with power through His Spirit in your
> inner self, [indwelling your innermost being and personality], so

that Christ *may dwell in your hearts* through your faith. And may you, having been [deeply] *rooted* and [securely] *grounded* in *love,* Be fully capable of comprehending with all the saints (God's people) the *width* and *length* and *height* and *depth* of *His love* [*fully experiencing that amazing, endless love*].

Ephesians 3:16-18 (AMP, italics added for emphasis)

This amazing love is available for all those who believe in Jesus. People who give their lives to Jesus are given a place at His table. If you haven't done this and long to experience this endless love, ask Him to come into your heart. In that moment, Jesus will create a place for you right next to Him at His table. I promise His love will change your life forever.

Nutrition Facts

I have included a Nutrition Facts label after each main course for you to see the nutritional qualities of each feast and how it may affect not only your body, but your mind and spirit as well. We all need our Daily Value of Christ!

Love Nutrition Label

Nutrition Facts

Unlimited servings per container

Serving size   **Overflowing cups**

Amount per serving

Christus

Consumption is a great source for
the following: % Daily Value*

Overwhelming sense of happiness	100%
Nourishment for body, soul, & spirit	100%
Removing an orphan mentality	100%
Ability to unconditionally love others	100%
Looking in the mirror and loving it	100%
Casting out fear	100%

*The % Daily Value (DV) tells you how much a nutrient in a serving contributes to a daily diet. Feasting on His Love every day is recommended for heavenly nutritional health.

I hope you enjoyed feasting on His love. Now it is time for dessert! I have created desserts for you to indulge in the Lord. You will need your utensils (a pencil and extra paper) and quiet time. Take this time to relish all that He is to you and for you. After each main course there will be dessert, so enjoy!

DESSERT

Love Ambush

I want you to find a friend, family member, coworker, or stranger and love ambush them with an encouraging word. It can be as simple as sending a text saying, "I was thinking about you and wanted you to know how much I value your kindness and wisdom." Or you can ask the Lord to highlight a stranger and then just go speak an encouraging word to them. I do this often in the grocery store. I'll ask the Lord to spotlight someone for me, and then I'll go up to them and love ambush them with what the Lord wants me to say. I often find myself encouraging the staff who work in the grocery stores.

Reflection Questions

I want you to take a minute and ask yourself these questions (and be honest). It will help you see how you feel about yourself and others.

> How do I see the Lord loving me? Write down examples throughout the day.
>
> How am I loving those around me? Write down specific examples of actions or words.

Are you convinced that nothing could separate you from God's love (Romans 8:38-39)? If yes, how are you convinced (list the evidence)? If no, why not? Be completely honest, then dig up love scriptures and post them all around you. Speak His love out loud every day.

DAY 2

FEAST ON HIS FINISHED WORK

> **Food for Thought**: What you eat nourishes your body. When we feast on Jesus, it nourishes our soul.

Therefore when Jesus had received the sour wine, He said, "It is finished!" And He bowed His head and gave up His spirit.

John 19:30 (NASB)

What is "It"?

I want you to know the importance and power of words as we start our main course today. Words can help you understand a deeper meaning. For example, let's look at the definition of the word "finished" from Merriam-Webster.com. In brackets, I've included some of my own clarifications.

> **Finished** (adjective)
> 1a. Entirely done [Not half done]
> 1b. Brought to a completed state [Not still a work in progress]
> 2. Marked by the highest quality: Consummate [Not missing anything]

As we feast today, I want you to recognize all that Jesus accomplished through His life, all that He *finished*!

One day, I was feasting on all that my Beloved had done for me, wondering about the "It" that Jesus finished. What is "It" that He finished? What does it include? Then I felt a sweet whisper say, "It is everything that was required to make you inseparable from the Father. I finished it all." There is no longer a barrier that blocks you from living in the fullness of God in any capacity. Jesus defeated the power of sin, the need for performance-oriented holiness, our broken identity, sickness, and more.

Dead to Sin and Alive to God

> So look upon *your old sin nature as dead* and *unresponsive to sin,* and instead be alive to God, alert to him, through Jesus Christ our Lord.
>
> Romans 6:11 (TLB, italics added for emphasis)

Jesus took your sinful self and co-crucified it with Himself on the cross, so that you can be in union with Him and alive to Him (Gal. 2:20). Galatians 2:20 and Romans 6:11 are verses of freedom! I recommend that you read Romans 6 in multiple translations. Let this chapter sink into your heart and mind. Sin no longer has any power over you. Romans 6:6 says, "Your old evil desires were nailed to the cross with him; that part of you that loves to sin was *crushed and fatally wounded*, so that your sin-loving body is no longer under sin's control, no longer needs to be a slave to sin" (TLB, italics added for emphasis). This means that you can live your life free from sin's bondage. You don't have to wait until you die to be free from the clutches of sin! This is the good news!

As we feast on His finished work, we start to recognize the little voice that comes into our mind, telling us that we will never break out of the cycles of sin—that we are broken and must persevere until heaven. This voice is a lie that tries to keep you out of a true relationship with the Lord. I'll mention more about this during our main course on Day 20: *Feast on His Freedom*, but let me say this: only free people can free people. If you are still bound to sin, how can you expect to see people break free from its grasp? Jesus showed us and told us that we can. Today is the day to feast on how Jesus freed you from the cycles of sin. He destroyed sin on the cross. Now, we get to live in that victory!

Jesus is Not My Employer

I used to think that my relationship with Christ depended on my performance. I thought that if I didn't pray or read the Bible for so many hours, I would never achieve the intimacy necessary to see His anointing in my life. What a lie that is! Your anointing to see and do the works of the Lord is not based on your performance. It is based on His. He already finished everything you need to see His anointing fall over your life. He just wants us to live life with Him. Jesus is not an employer evaluating a work performance report and handing out promotions based on your output. He is a lover, friend, confidante, and bridegroom.

I was in a conference back in 2018, listening to Georgian Banov speak about the cross and all that Jesus did for us. We were directed to read in Colossians 2, and I was reading verse 10, which says, "So you also are *complete* through your union with Christ, who is the head over every ruler and authority" (NLT, italics added for emphasis). The word, "complete" jumped off the page at me. I started thinking, *Wait, I'm not a 'work in progress'? I'm already complete? I don't have to wait for some special encounter to see the fullness of Jesus in my life? I have union with Him now—in this life?!* I started laughing in the joy of the Lord.

My perspective on Jesus completely shifted. I stopped focusing on my lack and started focusing on His fullness. I saw that what Jesus has, I have. He completed me. Past tense. There is no amount of work I can do today that will contribute to my salvation or gain me more favor with the Lord. He lavishes His favor on me just because I am in union with Him!

I hope that some weight has been lifted from you today. Feasting on Him helps us keep our eyes on Him. I like to marinate in His accomplishments because they bring unique flavors to my life. The longer I marinate, the more I look different, smell different, and become different.

Finished Work Nutrition Label

Nutrition Facts

Unlimited servings per container

Serving size   **Overflowing cups**

Amount per serving

Christ

Consumption is a great source for

the following: **% Daily Value***

Freedom from the tyranny of Sin	100%
Freedom from performance evangelism	100%
Seeing yourself as *complete* in Christ	100%
Understanding true union with Jesus	100%
Destroying the lies of the Enemy	100%
Overflowing in gratitude for all He did	100%

*The % Daily Value (DV) tells you how much a nutrient in a serving contributes to a daily diet. Feasting on His Finished Work every day is recommended for heavenly nutritional health.

DESSERT

Marinate with the Lamb

Read Romans 6 in at least five different translations and circle the words that represent Jesus' accomplishments, or that stand out to you. Write down your thoughts on the different translations. Reflect on how this chapter gives you the freedom to have a fuller life.

Reflection Questions

I want to pose the same question to you that I wrote about at the beginning of today's meal. What is "It" that Jesus finished? Write down your thoughts and how you could answer this question for someone else.

What does it look like to be dead to sin?

What does it look like to be alive to Christ?

Honesty time. Have you been seeing God as an employer who gives you more influence, anointing, and favor based on how much time and effort you put in? How do you see your perspective shifting after feasting on His finished work today?

DAILY SPECIALS

Lamb Marinated in New Wine

served with a heaping portion of joy and other Holy Spirit organic fruits

Bread of Life Sandwich

with 3-in-1 trinity protein special and smothered in an "it is finished" sauce

DAY 3

FEAST ON HIS JOY

Now go home and have a feast. Share your food and wine with those who don't have enough. Today is holy to our Lord, so don't be sad. The joy that the Lord gives you will make you strong.

Nehemiah 8:10 (GNT)

Strength in Joy

What is joy? I often see people confuse joy with happiness. Joy is not happiness. Joy can include happiness, but it is not dependent upon it. Happiness is an emotion that is fleeting, but joy is a state of being (ever-present and accessible) that comes when we say "yes" to Jesus. We are supposed to walk and live in joy because it is a fruit of the Spirit. It is so important that joy is listed second, right after love in Galatians 5:22-23! We often misunderstand how powerful joy is in our lives. Joy is not based on our circumstances or how we are feeling today. It is built on understanding Jesus' finished work and His victory.

Nehemiah 8:10 says that the joy of the Lord is strength. Let's look at the context of this verse. God had helped the remnant of Israel restore the city walls of Jerusalem and, by doing so, planted fear in the hearts of their enemies, who tried to stop the building of the wall. Once the wall was finished, the people of Israel gathered and listened as Ezra read the law of Moses. The people started weeping when they heard the law. Ezra told them not to worry or be sad (for their mistakes) but instead to focus on the Lord and celebrate His victory and redemption. Ezra knew that God did not want His people to wallow in their mistakes and failures. God wanted His people to feast and celebrate their new beginning with Him! With Jesus, we have a new beginning too!

The Lord wants us to know the strength of joy. Joy lifts the spirit and refocuses the mind. It fills our thoughts with encouragement and restores hope. It shifts our perspective to see that no matter what happens in life, Jesus is right there. Whether you are struggling emotionally, physically, or financially, He is right there. Joy comes and stays when we know that Jesus is the solution to *every* problem. The joy I am talking about is supernatural. It cannot be found outside of Jesus. It's like refreshing air that we breathe in. I often feel like joy is my oxygen. I can't live without it. I breathe it in, and it circulates throughout my entire body. I start laughing in the joy of the Lord!

Joy affects our perspective. I want you to understand that God is not a grumpy God. He is a joyful God. He does not look at you and see a mistake. He looks at you and sees His loving creation. He rejoices over you!

> The Lord your God is in the midst of you, a Mighty One, a Savior [Who saves]! *He will rejoice over you with joy*; He will rest [in silent satisfaction] and in His love He will be silent and *make no mention [of past sins, or even recall them]*; He will exult over you with singing.
>
> Zephaniah 3:17 (AMPC) (italics added for emphasis)

Wow! He will not mention or recall our past sins! That alone makes me want to stand up and celebrate! If God will not mention or recall our past sins, why do we feel the need to constantly reflect on them? Why do we allow them to fill our mind? These types of reflections are nothing but junk food. We need to stop eating junk food and start feasting on His joy!

Transformation in Joy

A joyful heart is good medicine, But a broken spirit dries up
the bones.

Proverbs 17:22 (NASB)

I want to share with you my testimony of how joy transformed my life. My husband and I moved to Japan in 2009 to be working missionaries at a school. We fell in love with Japan and loved working with students of all ages. We loved them and wanted them to know the love of Jesus.

We stayed for over seven years and, to be honest, got burned out. I had love, but I had no joy. I was tired. Tired of my husband being sick, tired of working long hours, tired of being in what I call a "spiritual black hole." I started to be plagued with guilt because I was even too tired to read my Bible!

Thank the Lord that He can move through us even when we don't have a great mindset. In spite of being burned out, we still saw God do miraculous things. In 2016, after our oldest daughter was born, God released James and I to move back to America. We decided to rest and not volunteer in any ministry for a while.

One day at church, I heard about a conference for living the supernatural life (the same one mentioned in Day 2). I felt my spirit jump. I wanted to go be with people who sought the "more" of the Lord—the greater things that Jesus mentioned (John 14:12-13). It was at this conference that I encountered joy. I went into this conference still burned out, but I left transformed in joy. Once I realized that Jesus wanted a relationship with me filled with intimacy and without performance, joy completely consumed me.

My husband is a witness to my joy transformation. He even told people he had a new wife. Ever since that "Jesus joy" encounter, I have never been the same. I realized the strength of joy. I realized I could live like I was dead to sin and alive with Christ now! Imagine a death row inmate being told that someone had fulfilled her sentence, and she was now free to go with no criminal record. She would leave the prison and run, jump, shout, and dance with joy! That's how I felt at that moment and how I've felt every day since. The joy of the Spirit is like a fountain planted inside me. It can never be uprooted or run out!

How do I know my transformation is real? When my family gets sick, when someone dies, when unexpected bills come, I rest in Jesus. I look to Him. I laugh with Him. I trust Him and know that no matter what happens, He is good. I expect Him to always help me. I delight in Him and He delights in me. "Splendor and majesty are in his presence. Strength and joy are where he is" (1 Chronicles 16:27, GW).

Joy is where the Lord is, and He lives in me! This means joy is all around me everywhere I go! As you feast on His joy, your life will change. Once you taste His joy, you will never be satisfied without it. One of the best ways to feast on His joy is to realize that Jesus already completed you. You don't have to strive to be perfect. You only need to rest in His perfection. When tough times come, focus on Jesus. His joy is your strength. He holds the solution to every problem. He is the one who protects us and keeps us safe from the Enemy. Don't let fear get into your mind and take root. Fear comes when we doubt God's ability to meet *every* need. You are not alone. There is nothing too big for Him to handle. True joy is resting in the arms of the Beloved.

Joy Nutrition Label

Nutrition Facts

Unlimited servings per container

Serving size **Overflowing cups**

Amount per serving

Christt

Consumption is a great source for

the following: **% Daily Value***

Uncontrollable laughter	100%
Uncontrollable dancing	100%
Strength in your body and mind	100%
Life transformation	100%
Supernatural optimism	100%
Supernatural expectation	100%

*The % Daily Value (DV) tells you how much a nutrient in a serving contributes to a daily diet. Feasting on His Joy every day is recommended for heavenly nutritional health.

DESSERT

Laugh at the Lies

For this activation I want you to read the following statements aloud and then laugh at them. They are lies and are as harmful as the worst type of junk food.

- God can't use me because of my past.
- I can't hear the voice of the Lord.
- I am a "work in progress."
- I am not gifted enough for the Lord to use me.
- I don't have the anointing of healing or prophecy.
- My worth is found in my works.
- I'm not a joyful person.
- I have to get my life in order to see the supernatural in my life.
- I've missed my chance for God to move through me.
- The severity of my sins can't be forgiven.

Reflection Questions

How do you see the joy of the Lord in your life? How do you showcase the joy of Jesus to those around you?

How do you shift your mind from problems to solutions? Write down three specific ways and put them somewhere you can see them every day.

DAY 4

FEAST ON HIS FAITH

Food for Thought: To feast on the Lord is to also take time digesting what He says.

Looking away [from all that will distract] to Jesus, Who is the *Leader and the Source of our faith* [giving the first incentive for our belief] and is also *its Finisher* [bringing it to maturity and perfection]. He, for the joy [of obtaining the prize] that was set before Him, endured the cross, despising and ignoring the shame, and is now seated at the right hand of the throne of God.

Hebrews 12:2 (AMPC, italics added for emphasis)

The Source of Faith

I grew up in church and, for the longest time, believed that God moving through me depended on my faith. It was all about Paula's faith level. I would pray for healing, and if it didn't happen, I would think, *I must not have had enough faith.* Or *I need to press into the Lord so He can give me more faith.* I was always so self-focused.

After understanding Jesus' finished work, I started to realize how often I was looking at myself and my lack instead of looking at Him and His fullness. I used to only see my deficit of faith, and now I see that I possess *His* faith. He is the source of faith! I don't have to worry about my progression of faith anymore. I live in His full and complete faith. I have the faith *of* Christ. Galatians 2:20 reveals how our new life is lived by the faith *of* Jesus. "I am crucified with Christ: nevertheless I live; yet not I, but Christ liveth in me: and the life which I now live in the flesh I live by *the faith of the Son of God,* who loved me and gave himself for me" (KJV, italics added for emphasis). We have a new life with a new faith. Let's relish that for a moment. Christ lives in you! It doesn't say with you or around you, but *in* you. If He lives in you, don't you think that His faith does too?

I love to read multiple translations because they can bring about different revelations. For example, let's read Galatians 3:25 in the NASB, "But now *that faith* has come, we are no longer under a guardian" (italics added for emphasis). Now let's read it in the TLB, "But now *that Christ* has come, we don't need those laws any longer to guard us and lead us to him" (italics added for emphasis). This translation changes the word 'faith' to 'Christ!' Let's read one more of the same verse in the Montgomery New Testament, "But now that *the Faith* is come, we are no longer under a tutor-slave" (italics added for emphasis). This version capitalizes Faith because it represents Christ! Christ is the substance of our faith because He is the Source and Finisher of our faith (Hebrews 11:1 and 12:2).

We need to feast upon and savor the faith of Christ because He is where our faith flows from! He is where faith originates and where it finds maturity. We need to stop thinking that we must strive for more faith. Instead, let's rest in the arms of our Beloved. He has all the faith we will ever need.

Spreading Faith

Now that we see where our faith originates, let's talk about spreading faith in the world around us. Many people came to Jesus and received healing. He also commented a few times about certain people having great faith. Does that mean that Jesus was impressed by their own ability to have faith? No, Jesus was impressed that they believed in *Him* and completely trusted *Him*.

Faith is comprised of belief and trust. Every time I sit down, I have faith that the chair I'm sitting on will hold me without breaking. Everyone has faith in something. The people who had great faith in the Gospels understood that Jesus was the source. They heard about Him, and faith came! "Faith comes from hearing, that is, hearing the Good News about Christ" (Romans 10:17, NLT). Even in this verse you see that Christ is the source of faith because hearing about Him results in faith. True faith is all about Him, not us. When we share the good news of Jesus, we are creating atmospheres for faith to dwell!

There are so many stories of Jesus encountering people who recognized Him as their answer because they heard testimonies about Him and believed the reports. These testimonies about Jesus were like seeds planted in the hearts of the people who heard them. Faith spread and blossomed within them. Even today, people are encouraged when we testify of healing and other wonderful things He is doing in our lives. The faith of Jesus is ignited within them. They start to believe for more.

We see a wonderful example of this in Acts 14:8-10. In this passage of the Bible, Paul was preaching and a man, crippled from birth, was listening to him. Paul looked at the man and realized he had the faith to be healed. Paul then told him to stand up and the man received his healing! How did this man get the faith to be healed? He heard the good news and faith came! He didn't spend hours begging God for more faith. He didn't try to earn more faith by working for the Lord. He just simply heard the good news, believed, and trusted that it was true. We need to understand that Jesus is who He says He is. Trust that He will do what He says He will do, and watch faith expand.

Here is another morsel about faith to chew on: Jesus even heals when the person needing the healing doesn't have faith. What!? Yes, people were healed and are healed today, even when they do not have faith for it. Let's look at an example in the Bible. In John 5:5-9 there was a man who had been sick for 38 years. Jesus went to Him and asked him if he wanted to get well. The man answered Jesus, saying that he had no one to help him into the pool and that others always got in before him. I don't see any hope or faith in this man's answer, but Jesus heals him anyway! This man was not healed because of his personal faith, but the faith of Jesus. This is something that gets me so excited! That same faith is what I get to operate in for healing!

Once, when we were still living in Japan, we went out to worship and pray on the streets at night. We set up near restaurants and bars where we knew people would be drinking the night away. Right in the middle of praying for people and worshipping, a Japanese man came up to us. He was a member of the mafia and was bothered that we were disrupting business. Well, one of the people with us got a healing word of knowledge for him and asked if we could pray for him. He looked at us like we were crazy. He told us that we could pray and once nothing happened, we were to leave the area. Of course, we agreed because my friends knew Jesus would heal him. That's exactly what happened. He was healed. He started jumping and making so much noise in celebration that he started "disrupting" people! Then he started to testify, and faith spread.

I tell this story because this man did not have any faith in Jesus. He did not believe in Jesus, like Jesus, or want Jesus. But Jesus believed in him. I also didn't have faith-filled thoughts while praying for this man. I was thinking, *Lord, you have to heal this man; if not, we are going to have to leave this place!* My thoughts may not have been overflowing with faith at that moment, but the faith of Jesus was all that was needed to see this man healed. I have learned to rest in the faith of Jesus to see people healed. When I lay my hands on someone for prayer, I imagine three people with me. God the Father is the big guy right behind me. Jesus is on my side with His hands right over mine, and the Holy Spirit is on my other side with fire to flow out and consume any affliction. I never see myself alone. If you have Jesus, you already have all the faith you need to see people healed.

However, that doesn't mean that we are satisfied. How do we grow in faith? Grow closer to Jesus. There is always more of Jesus becoming visible in us. His faith included.

Faith Nutrition Label

Nutrition Facts

Unlimited servings per container

Serving size   **Overflowing cups**

Amount per serving

Christ

Consumption is a great source for the following: **% Daily Value***

Realizing you have the faith of Jesus	100%
Seeing your faith as complete in Him	100%
Creating an atmosphere of faith	100%
Learning about the source of faith	100%
Being activated in healing	100%
Freedom from striving for faith	100%

*The % Daily Value (DV) tells you how much a nutrient in a serving contributes to a daily diet. Feasting on His Faith every day is recommended for heavenly nutritional health.

DESSERT

Power Sandwich

I want you to close your eyes and imagine that you are completely surrounded by God the Father, Jesus, and the Holy Spirit. You are in the middle of a power sandwich. Power is all around you. Jesus is the bread, God the Father is the meat, the Holy Spirit is the sauce. You are the filling. You are completely smothered by all three. You cannot move without them moving. You are four parts but one sandwich. When you go to the grocery store, work, school, church, or home, they do too. They are a part of you. They are your source for everything you need, and don't forget that there is always more.

Reflection Questions

What were two things that impacted you from the feast today? Why did they impact you?

How does knowing that Jesus is the source and finisher of your faith change your thoughts about faith?

Challenge: Reflect on the faith of Jesus this week and then go pray for at least 2 people for healing. Write down what happens.

DAY 5

FEAST ON HIS HEALING

> **Food for Thought:** There is a saying that goes, "You are what you eat." My goal is to be just like Jesus.

Jesus traveled throughout the region of Galilee, teaching in the synagogues and announcing the Good News about the Kingdom. And he healed every kind of disease and illness. News about him spread as far as Syria, and people soon began bringing to him all who were sick. And whatever their sickness or disease, or if they were demon possessed or epileptic or paralyzed—*he healed them all.*

Matthew 4:23-24 (NLT, italics added for emphasis)

God's Will on Display

Whenever I read about Jesus, I see His life as the will of God being showcased for all to see. Everywhere Jesus went, He preached good news! He preached and demonstrated salvation, love, provision, restoration, healing, and more. It seems like everywhere Jesus went, people were healed. I love this because it shows us with evidence that God's will is to see people healed. I never see Jesus leaving someone sick who came to Him in the

Bible. In fact, He healed *all* who came to Him. He never said to anyone, "I can't heal you because God doesn't want you healed right now." He never said, "Oh no, I can't heal you because you need this sickness to grow stronger in character and faith." He healed *all* that came to Him, every time. Let's take a moment and relish some of the evidence.

> As the sun went down that evening, people throughout the village brought sick family members to Jesus. No matter what their diseases were, the touch of his hand healed *every one*.
>
> Luke 4:40 (NLT, italics added for emphasis)

> And the whole multitude sought to touch Him, for power went out from Him and healed them *all*.
>
> Luke 6:19 (NKJV, italics added for emphasis)

> But a lot of people found out about this and followed him. Jesus welcomed them. He spoke about God's kingdom and healed *everyone* who was sick.
>
> Luke 9:11 (CEV, italics added for emphasis)

> When evening had come, they brought to Him many who were demon-possessed. And He cast out the spirits with a word, and healed *all* who were sick.
>
> Matthew 8:16 (NKJV, italics added for emphasis)

> Then Jesus went about all the cities and villages, teaching in their synagogues, preaching the gospel of the kingdom, and healing *every sickness and every disease* among the people.
>
> Matthew 9:35 (NKJV, italics added for emphasis)

These verses I listed are not the only ones, but you get a taste of God's will as represented in Jesus. See, we don't have to wonder what God's will or timing is when it comes to healing because Jesus demonstrated it for us! I am flooded with joy when I think about it. God demonstrated that He wants me healthy. He wants me whole! So why do people not always get healed if it is always God's will to heal? Great question. Let's continue to feast on His healing and discover more.

Jesus spoke on God's will for us in John 10:10, "The thief approaches with malicious intent, looking to steal, slaughter, and destroy; I came to give life with joy and abundance" (VOICE). Some translate "abundance" as "fullness of life." How can we have a fullness in life if we are left in our sickness? It is the Enemy's will that wants you destroyed in your sickness—physically, mentally, and spiritually. Whenever I pray for people and they do not get healed in that moment, I never doubt God's will to heal or His timing. I sit at His table, rest my head on His shoulder, and ask Him for more of Himself. I also say to Jesus, "When You were physically here on this earth, all who came to You were healed, so show me how to become just like You." I don't excuse it as "God's will" when I don't see someone healed right then. Instead, I feast on the Healer because the more I partake of Him, the more I become like Him. There is a power and boldness that comes upon us when we believe that God heals and wants everyone healed today. We pray from victory, not doubt. Wondering if it is God's will to heal is a form of doubt. Instead of snacking on junk food like doubt, let's feast on the evidence of Jesus displaying God's will as He healed them all.

Experience Healing

First off, your healing is already paid for in full. 1 Peter 2:24 says, "And He Himself brought our sins in His body up on the cross, so that we might die to sin and live for righteousness; by His wounds you *were* healed" (NASB, italics added for emphasis). What does this mean? It means that your healing was already accomplished on the cross. So how do we experience it? We keep our attention and position towards Jesus.

When my husband was 14, he was diagnosed with Crohn's Disease. He struggled with it for over 20 years. It was hard for me to watch him curl up in a ball in so much agony, begging God to heal him time and time again. It was hard watching as he even asked God to put him out of his misery and take him to heaven. But God. Today my husband lives pain free and with miracle intestines. For years during our journey of understanding healing, I questioned God. I doubted God. I blamed God. I'm so glad that He is so filled with love for me even when I threw my tantrums! We started to see healing in our lives when we experienced intimacy with the Lord. My husband went from seeing himself as broken, worthless, and guilt-ridden to seeing himself as Jesus sees him—priceless, whole, and pure. We feasted on the truth as it is written in the Word. We feasted on Jesus. We stopped only reading *about* Him and started being in a relationship *with* Him. Joy flooded our minds, and joy brings healing and transformation (Day 3).

> **Note: Laughter is scientifically proven to bring health benefits!
> I'll talk more about that when we eat Dessert.** **

You see, we experienced healing when we started to experience relationship with Jesus. We talked with Jesus. We listened to Jesus. We discussed and included Jesus in our plans. We trusted in Jesus when things were hard. We rejoiced with Him because though sorrow may last through the night, joy comes in the morning (Psalm 30:5). It was like heaven invaded our house and there is no sickness in heaven! Just being in His presence is healing, and we can be in His presence everywhere because He lives in us.

Jesus doesn't want to just visit people; He wants to inhabit people. "Then Christ will *make his home in your hearts* as you trust in him. Your roots will grow down into God's love and keep you strong" (Ephesians 3:17, NLT, italics added for emphasis). Christ makes you strong. He will ground you in God's love. This changes everything when we are faced with sickness, death, disasters, and disappointment. I don't focus my eyes on the problems. I focus my eyes on the Healer and then feast on His healing.

The other side to experiencing healing is God using you to heal others. Jesus said that He does what He sees His Father doing. We are the same. We do what we see Jesus doing. The more time we spend with Jesus, the more healing flows out of us. My husband and I are so joyful when we pray for the sick. We have this joy in healing because we know Jesus has the victory and He is the Healer. I pray from victory. I know that when I pray for someone, something happens. Jesus commissioned me and you to heal the sick, raise the dead, and cast out demons (Matthew 10:8). Healing is supposed to be a part of our everyday life.

That's why I sit at His table and feast on His healing. I don't just want to hear about healing or know about it. I want to consume it. I want it to become a part of me so that I can release it to others. I have never experienced so much healing in and through my life as I do today. I pray for the sick and afflicted, and they get healed because Jesus lives in me and we walk out life together. If you want to experience the joy of seeing Jesus heal others through you, feast on Him and His Word. We often become more like those we spend time with. That's why I like to spend time with Jesus. I want to be just like Him.

Extra Table Discussion: Words as Seeds

I love healing. My heart's passion is for all people to be healed and for diseases such as cancer to be eradicated. I want Jesus to get what He paid for on the cross, which includes our healing. One day I was reading with the Lord in the Message, and Proverbs 18:21 seemed to jump off the page. "Words kill, words give life; they're either poison or fruit—you choose." I started to imagine that inside every person there is a garden. Every word they hear plants some kind of seed. Each seed will grow some type of crop. There are good crops and there are bad crops.

With each word we speak to someone, we plant a seed. Are they seeds that bring good crops such as freedom, joy, peace, and love? Or are they seeds that bring bad crops such as anxiety, fear, shame, guilt, and worthlessness? Are we healing people with our words or destroying them? I started to pay attention to how I spoke to my husband, my kids, and my friends. I wanted to plant seeds of life.

I present this table discussion because it can greatly affect health and wholeness. God knows how powerful our words are. That is why He had Solomon write about it in Proverbs. Experiencing healing also includes speaking life into people. Negative words are scientifically proven to cause physical ailments such as stress, anxiety, sleep deprivation, and more. Positive words are also scientifically proven to affect areas of our brain and calm our bodies. Take time and pay attention to your words. Many afflictions and diseases have roots that stem from some form of verbal trauma. If we recognize the power of our words, we can not only see the sick healed but prevent sickness from ever taking root.

With the power of His Holy Spirit, we have been given protection over our gardens as well. I tell my kids and all the people I teach, "If it doesn't sound like Jesus, feel like Jesus, or look like Jesus, you don't have to let it in." I just dump it into my spiritual trash can. I don't let it even get planted.

What you plant will grow. Which will you choose?

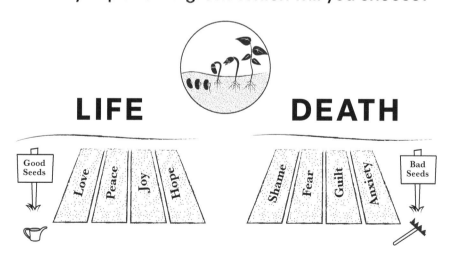

LIFE   DEATH

Good Seeds — Love · Peace · Joy · Hope

Shame · Fear · Guilt · Anxiety — Bad Seeds

Healing Nutrition Label

Nutrition Facts

Unlimited servings per container

Serving size   Overflowing cups

Amount per serving

Christ

Consumption is a great source

for the following: % Daily Value*

Getting excited by Jesus healing ALL	100%
Experiencing healing	100%
Understanding the power of words	100%
Jesus inhabiting you	100%
Seeing others healed through you	100%
Experiencing joy in healing	100%

---

*The % Daily Value (DV) tells you how much a nutrient in a serving contributes to a daily diet. Feasting on His Healing every day is recommended for heavenly nutritional health.

DESSERT

Core Truth

[1]Psychology Today defines Core Truth: "Our Core Truths are *repeating patterns of thought and behavior* defined by our various assumptions and expectations, as well as our ideas about the way the world works, collected over time." Our Core Truths cannot be swayed. They will stand with you even amongst persecution, rejection, and evidence to the contrary.

What are your core truths about healing? (Example: God is good) Write down three of your core truths when it comes to healing.

1. _____

2. _____

3. _____

Laughter Heals

Proverbs 17:22:

A happy heart is good medicine and a joyful mind causes healing,
But a broken spirit dries up the bones. (AMP)

Being cheerful keeps you healthy. It is slow death to be gloomy all
the time. (GNT)

---

1 Psychology Today https://www.psychologytoday.come/us/blog/enlightenedlving/200808/core-truths-core-beliefs-and-obstacles-progress-pt-2

I hope you are ready to laugh because laughing brings healing in many ways. Let me list some of them:

Physical Benefits	Mental Benefits	Social Benefits
Lowers your stress hormones	Enhances mood	Builds up relationships
Burns calories	Reduces anxiety	Improves team unity
Heart disease preventative	Keeps joy in your life	Brings people together
Relaxes muscles	Relieves stress	Helps others feel at ease
Alleviates pain	Breaks anger strongholds	Can help calm tension
Boosts Immune System	Strengthens mental resilience	Showcases the joy of the Lord

Now that we see some of the benefits of laughter, I want you to laugh today even if you don't feel like it. I want you to write your own Lies to Laugh At (Day 3). Then *laugh* at them. Laugh at the absurdity of the Enemy and his lies.

Reminder: Want a recipe from the Chef? At His table the Chef always gives the recipes for free.

DAY 6

FEAST ON HIS WORD

Food for Thought: Do most people think eating is a lot of work? No. Is this one reason why Jesus said to eat Him?

For the Word that God speaks is *alive* and *full of power* [making it *active, operative, energizing,* and *effective*]; it is sharper than any two-edged sword, penetrating to the dividing line of the breath of life (soul) and [the immortal] spirit, and of joints and marrow [of the deepest parts of our nature], exposing and sifting and analyzing and judging the very thoughts and purposes of the heart.

Hebrews 4:12 (AMPC, italics added for emphasis)

The Sword

The Word of God is inherently powerful because all Scripture is breathed by God (2 Timothy 3:16). The Spirit of God indwells the Word. This is why Hebrews 4:12 tells us that the Word of God is alive and full of power. How many times have you read the Word and felt an emotion or felt your spirit jump within you? It is because God is speaking directly to you. He is speaking about you in His Word. When we speak the Word out, we are actively releasing the power of God. His Word is like a sword. In

Ephesians 6:17, we are told that the Word is our sword. "And you will need the helmet of salvation and the sword of the Spirit—which is the Word of God" (TLB).

I'm so glad that swords are both offensive and defensive. This means that as we feast on His Word, we start to sharpen our sword, which will not only defend us when the Enemy tries to destroy us but also arm us to go on the offensive to break down strongholds. I don't know about you, but I used to get tired of always feeling like I was on the defensive in my life. I felt like the Enemy was always attacking health, finances, emotions, and relationships. I used to pray and ask God for help (which is what we are supposed to do), but as He gently pointed out to me, I have a weapon that He has given me—His Word. I started to consume it. I digested it. It nourished my heart, mind, and body. It felt like I was in sword training. I would read the Word, and it was like God was teaching me battle techniques. I wanted to become an expert swordswoman. I wanted to wield His Word with precision, but to do that, I had to know what it says and the context behind it. I started looking at whole chapters instead of just one or two verses so that I could grasp His Word for myself. I wanted the fullness of His Word, not just bite-sized morsels.

"Let the word of the Anointed One richly inhabit your lives. With all wisdom teach, counsel, and instruct one another" Colossians 3:16a, (VOICE). We need the Word to inhabit us. It is not enough to just know the Word of God; we need it to occupy our hearts. We speak from what is in our hearts (Matthew 12:34). What do you have in your heart? Do you have His Word as your daily bread? Are you eating it every day? Are you letting it nourish every part of you?

I have great news for you either way. Today is a great day to feast! Sit at His table, open your Bible, and ask Him to feed you from it. Take the passages that move your heart and write them down. Read them over and over. Absorb them. His Word is a love letter to you. Let His Word shape you. This is one of the many benefits of your "sword training." A swordsman's training changes his body and his mind. It is the same with the Word. It renews your mind (Romans 12:2), and it gives life (Psalm 119:50). It shows you the heart of the Father and all He wants to unveil within you.

Truth vs. Fact

After absorbing more and more of His Word, I started to recognize the differences between facts and truth. In the beginning was the Word (John 1:1), and the Word became flesh and full of truth (John 1:14). Jesus is what I call my "true north," or the main dish of my life. Basically, He is where I always direct my steps and keep my gaze fixed because then I will never go off course or be left empty. He is my Truth. He is the Word made flesh. Facts are not the truth if they do not align with the Word of God. The Enemy will use facts to try to move you away from Jesus and take your eyes off Him. Now, facts can become your truth if you align with them. What does this mean? I'm going to share my story as an example.

While living in Japan, my husband and I found out that we were infertile. *Fact:* We would not be able to have children naturally. *Truth:* Infertility was defeated at the cross by the blood of Jesus (Matthew 8:17). *Truth:* All things are possible with God (Matthew 19:26). My husband stood on those truths. I did for a while, but after seven years of constant failed attempts to become pregnant, that fact started to become my truth. I believed that we could not get pregnant. I blamed God. I was angry, frustrated, and bitter. All this while ministering in Japan. Disappointment had become a bad fruit in my spirit, and it was killing me. James would keep speaking the truth, but I didn't even want to hear it because I had become so offended at God.

For two years I lived in that place of offense, believing the facts over the truth of His Word. Then one day, I was so tired of hating my life, hating my circumstances, hating how I always felt angry, that I went to God and yelled, cried, and let the nasty stuff out of my heart. I stopped hiding my true feelings although I was supposed to be a good Christian woman. I just let them all out. God is so patient and loving with us! Here I was, yelling at Him so much that I collapsed on the bathroom floor in exhaustion and desperation.

Suddenly, I heard Him tell me how much He loves me. It didn't matter that I was offended and angry. It didn't matter that I had stopped believing in His Word. He was right there to pick me up and seat me right next to Him again. God healed my heart and restored my hope in that moment. I told Him how sorry I was for everything I had said and done. I realized His goodness is not dependent on me having children. I chose to praise Him even if I didn't get what I wanted. I just wanted to be with Him and have joy in Him again. Three months after I rested on Jesus and devoured the truth of His Word, I was pregnant. The facts that did not align with the Word disappeared, and the truth became our reality. We now have two beautiful daughters. Two miracles! My daughters are walking testaments of truth vs. facts to me. When I hear facts about sickness or financial problems, I look at my daughters and see how God's truth is victorious.

Don't misunderstand me. I am grateful for doctors and other professionals that can recognize and state the facts. I do not deny that the facts are real, but that does not mean I'm going to allow them to become my truth and take root in my mind and heart again. I like to know facts because they allow me to target my prayers. Facts are like little bull's-eyes to me. When I hear them and they do not align with the Word, I start speaking the truth and using my sword to cut them down. The more I sit at the Lord's table and feast on His Word, the more I consume the truth. I get it into my core. I don't just read or listen to the truth. I eat it. I take it inside of me. I believe it with all that I am. This is how we can live a life filled with joy no matter what facts come our way. The truth will make you free. "Then Jesus said to those Jews who believed Him, 'If you abide in My word, you are My disciples indeed. And you shall know the truth, and the *truth shall make you free*'" (John 8:31-32, NKJV, italics added for emphasis). It not only sets you free but makes you free.

I want to share one more example with you about my mom. She was diagnosed with breast cancer, which is a fact. However, she immediately started to speak the truth from the Word. Jesus heals. Cancer was defeated at the cross. She did not let the fact that she had cancer become her truth. She did not let cancer become a giant in her life or her mind. She did not fall into depression or anxiety over it. She rested on Jesus. She feasted on His Word. She kept her eyes on Him and who He says He is. She was so encouraged when she told me of her diagnosis that I was thinking, *Do you really have cancer?* It still brings tears to my eyes thinking about how filled she was with peace because she knew Jesus was her truth. My mom was made free from cancer by the truth found in Jesus.

Now, some have asked me, "What about when people die from cancer; then what?" The answer: God is still good. Jesus is the Healer. I may not understand why some die and some get healed, but I know that Jesus' blood killed cancer on the cross. Period. I will never let my life's experiences lower the power of His Word. When I pray for people and they do not get healed the way I expected or wanted, I don't doubt the truth of the Word just because my *experience* tells me healing didn't happen. I don't doubt that Jesus heals them all (Day 5). I sit at His table, lean on Him, and ask Him for more. I want my experiences to line up with the truth of His Word.

The Word Nutrition Label

Nutrition Facts

Unlimited servings per container

Serving size   **Overflowing cups**

Amount per serving

Christi

Consumption is a great source

for the following   **% Daily Value***

Powering up your spirit	100%
Understanding truth vs. facts	100%
Advancing the kingdom of heaven	100%
Becoming an expert with THE sword	100%
Mind transformation	100%
Love ambushes from Jesus	100%

*The % Daily Value (DV) tells you how much a nutrient in a serving contributes to a daily diet. Feasting on His Word every day is recommended for heavenly nutritional health.

DESSERT

Two Truths and a Fact

I want you to do a Truth vs. Fact interaction. Write down one negative personal fact. It could be a negative fact relating to health, finances, resources, etc. Then write down *two* truths from the Word that combat that fact. After you write them down, speak the truth aloud. Use your sword! Remember faith comes from hearing the Word.

Reflection Questions

Are you feasting on His Word or are you just reading it? Let me explain what I mean. To read something is to gain information. To feast on something is to intake it into your body where it can disperse nutrients. When you read the Word, is it changing you? How?

How can you go on the offensive with the Word in various parts of your life (work, school, family, church)?

Note: All meals prepared at this table are prepared without man-made preservatives and are Allergen-Free!

DAY 7

FEAST ON HIS GRACE

> **Food for Thought:** When people speak badly about themselves, do they know they are speaking about Jesus' favorite?

In our union with Christ Jesus, he raised us up with him to rule with him in the heavenly world. He did this to demonstrate for all time to come the *extraordinary greatness* of his grace in the love he showed us in Christ Jesus. For it is *by God's grace that you have been saved through faith*. It is *not the result of your own efforts*, but God's gift, so that no one can boast about it.

Ephesians 2:6-9 (GNT, italics added for emphasis)

Definitions of Grace

Today's spiritual meal is served with some extra spices. We are going to take a moment and savor some of the Biblical definitions of Grace (*charis* in Greek [2]G5485).

Divine influence upon the heart	That which affords joy, pleasure, and delight	God's favor given to those undeserving	Freedom from a debt

---

2   Sourced from The New Strong's Expanded Exhaustive Concordance of the Bible Red Letter Ed.

Divine influence upon the heart: God loves you so much that He wanted to put you in a position where He can directly influence your heart. Another word for influence is inspiration. You have God's inspiration written on your heart! The Lord Himself comes and moves your heart. His influence is how we can supernaturally love people. It is how we can supernaturally believe in the impossible. It is His divine influence on you that gives you the ability to see people the way Jesus sees them and impact the world.

That which affords joy, pleasure, and delight: Grace allows us to participate in the joy, pleasure, and delight of the Lord! His grace comes with blessing after blessing, which include joy, pleasure, and delight. John 1:16-17 says, "Out of the fullness of his grace he has blessed us all, giving us one blessing after another. God gave the law through Moses, but grace and truth came through Jesus Christ" (GNT). When was the last time you sat and thought about how the Lord delights in you? Imagine that grace is like a gift given to you. Once you open it, you have the key that gives you full access to the throne room of heaven. As the door to the throne room opens, joy, pleasure, and delight fill you up because you are now able to enter. God's delight in seeing you there just keeps washing over you. I've said this before: God is not a grumpy God. He enjoys you and He wants you to take pleasure in all He has for you through His grace.

God's favor given to those undeserving: Did you know that you have God's favor when you believe in Jesus? You have the favor of the Almighty One even though you can't do anything to deserve it. His favor means that He likes you. He supports you. He gives you preferential treatment. To be favored means to be set apart and treated as special. That is what His grace gives you. God's favor is not tied to your effort or you working for Him. If we could earn God's favor with our works, was Jesus' sacrifice really necessary? For years, Israel tried to work for their salvation. They kept having to try to make themselves worthy and clean. Now, the only question I have for you is, do you see yourself as special and favored in God's eyes? Because if you don't, then you need to feast more on His grace and let it be fully absorbed inside of you. "But if it is by grace (*His unmerited favor* and graciousness), it is no longer conditioned on works or anything men have done. Otherwise, grace would no longer be grace [it would be meaningless]" (Romans 11:6, AMPC, italics added for emphasis).

Freedom from a debt: Grace=Freedom. Jesus came to set you free. Free from everything that comes between you and the Father. He came because of God's grace and love. God did not want us shackled to sin anymore. He wanted us released from the grip and the voice of sin. *"Sin is no longer your master*, for you no longer live under the requirements of the law. Instead, you *live under the freedom of God's grace"* (Romans 6:14, NLT, italics added for emphasis). In multiple translations, sin is described as a master. Masters have voices. As slaves to sin, we could never get away from the voice of sin speaking into our mind and heart. But no longer do we have to even acknowledge the voice of sin because God's grace has made us completely free!

Note: Grace is not a license to sin. Though Jesus severs the ties from our old master of sin, we can choose to follow it again and our lifestyle will reflect which master we serve.

> What are we to do, then? Should we sin to our heart's content since there's no law to condemn us anymore? What a terrible thought! Don't you realize that grace frees you to choose your own master? But choose carefully, for you surrender yourself to become a servant—bound to the one you choose to obey. If you choose to love sin, it will become your master, and it will own you and reward you with death. But if you choose to love and obey God, he will lead you into perfect righteousness.
>
> Roman 6:15-16 (TPT)

His Grace Justifies

We just read how grace is freedom, but I want us to marinate in this freedom some more. What does it mean to be justified by grace? Imagine you were suddenly taken into a courtroom for judgement. You *are* guilty. There is a mountain of evidence that proves your guilt. Unexpectedly, the Judge looks at you and says, "I find you not guilty. Someone else already paid for *all* of your crimes. You are free."

Jesus dying on the cross for our sins is how grace justifies us. We get declared "not guilty" from *the* Judge. "For all have sinned and fall short of the glory of God, and are justified by his grace as a gift, through the redemption that is in Christ Jesus" (Romans 3:23-24, ESV). Savor that for a moment. You are not guilty. There are no charges against you anymore. They don't even exist anymore. His grace cleans your sin record. His grace washes the taint of sin off you. "For by the blood of Christ we are set free, that is, our sins are forgiven. How great is the grace of God" (Ephesians 1:7, GNT). His rich grace gifted you a seat at His table, so feast until you overflow!

One last note for this feast: the root word for *charis* is *chairō* ([3]G5463), which means to rejoice and thrive. In other words, the main ingredient for grace is rejoicing! God rejoices over you so much that He sent us Jesus to not only save us but also to see us thrive with Him.

---

[3]   Sourced from The New Strong's Expanded Exhaustive Concordance of the Bible Red Letter Ed.

Grace Nutrition Label

Nutrition Facts

Unlimited servings per container

Serving size　　　　**Overflowing cups**

Amount per serving

Christ

Consumption is a great source for

the following:　　　**% Daily Value***

Being under divine influence	100%
Being debt free from sin	100%
Overwhelming sense of delight	100%
Identifying as God's favorite	100%
Random eruptions of laughter in joy	100%
FREEDOM!!!!	100%

*The % Daily Value (DV) tells you how much a nutrient in a serving contributes to a daily diet. Feasting on His Grace every day is recommended for heavenly nutritional health.

DESSERT

Clean Slate

Often, we are quick to tell others or ourselves our faults. I want you to shift your thinking and focus on your assets. You have a clean slate. Just like we saw during our meal today, there is no more record of your wrongdoings. Jesus made you blameless. Take a moment and think about things you do that are good. Things you excel at which bless people. Write down as many as you can. Read them. Read them again. God wants to use your clean slate to empower the world.

Reflection Questions

How do you see God delighting in you?

Take a moment and reflect on the definitions for Grace. Based on your life's experiences, how would you define God's grace?

In what ways does grace help you live a life of rejoicing? Thriving? Write down your thoughts.

DAY 8

FEAST ON HIS PRESENCE

Food for Thought: We need to marinate in His presence. There is no microwavable food at His table.

What pleasure fills those who live every day in your temple, enjoying you as they worship in your presence!

Psalm 84:4 (TPT)

Fullness of Life

Wherever the presence of the Lord is, there is fullness of life. David recognized how the presence of God was complete sustenance for daily living. How did David get into the Lord's presence? He worshipped Him. David constantly reflected on the glory of God. We see this in his psalms. Here is one of my favorite verses: "You have let me experience the joys of life and the exquisite pleasures of your own eternal presence" (Psalm 16:11, TLB). David spent time with the Lord. Alone. He made time for God, and he was able to experience the pleasures of His presence. I want more of that! As I was spending time alone with the Lord and basking in His presence, I decided to share something with you that I wrote during my feast with Him:

The Presence of the Beloved

I come before You, my Beloved, and all else disappears from my vision. I cannot see anything but You. Just being in Your presence is like taking my very first breath, the day my life began. It is a fragrance that, once breathed in, infuses vitality throughout every part of my being. All things are possible in Your presence. The brilliance of Your presence surrounds me like a hand-tailored garment. It brings warmth to my soul. It comforts my heart. It focuses my thoughts on You. Your presence is like a mighty streak of lightning that flashes through my spirit, igniting a fire in its wake. It's like thunder that roars in my mind to awaken the dreams You have weaved for me. Your presence is where glory is defined and showcased. Signs and wonders emanate from You like a wave on the vast ocean of Your beauty. Your presence is where I can clearly hear Your voice. I hear the whispers of love that You save only for me. Your presence erases all anxiety, fear, and darkness, replacing it with hope, peace, and joy! Your presence is the embodiment of celebration because You removed my cage of corruption that separated us. Your presence is the origin of light and limitless expectations. There is no beginning or end in Your presence. There is just infinite love. Your presence is the fullness of life because You are here.

Thank You, Lord. Thank you for showing me who You are and who I am in You.

Dwelling Place

When we worship God in spirit and in truth, we enter His presence. We do not have to be in a building or a certain location to enter His presence. It is about our heart connecting to His heart. Our spirit connecting to His Spirit.

It's who you are and the way you live that count before God. Your worship must engage your spirit in the pursuit of truth. That's the kind of people the Father is out looking for: those who are simply and honestly themselves before him in their worship. God is sheer being itself—Spirit. Those who worship him must do it out of their very being, their spirits, their true selves, in adoration.

John 4:23-24 (MSG)

His presence is all around you because He is in you. "Jesus answered, 'If anyone loves me, he will keep my word. My Father will love him, and we will come to him and *make our home with him*'" (John 14:23, CSB, italics added for emphasis). When we accept Jesus, we make a home for the Lord. He comes and fills up His house (you) with His presence. Let that digest for a moment. You don't have to go anywhere to be closer to God! God wanted you from the beginning of time. You. When sin corrupted God's creation, He couldn't come close to us because He would destroy us. His holiness cannot dwell in the same space as corruption. God longed for us to encounter His rich, expansive, complete presence so that our life would be whole.

In the Old Testament we see God's presence come into the Tent of Meeting. Exodus 40:34 says, "Then the cloud [the Shekinah, God's visible, dwelling presence] covered the Tent of Meeting, and the glory and brilliance of the LORD filled the tabernacle" (AMP). God covered the Tent and then His glory filled it. You are now the Tent of Meeting. His brilliance and glory now cover you. The Lord was tired of having a veil in between you and Him. He wanted to see you clearly and intimately, so you would no longer be separated from each other's presence. He wanted complete and absolute union.

I hope you are ready for the continuation of this cuisine, because tomorrow we are going to completely indulge on His intimacy.

Presence Nutrition Label

Nutrition Facts

Unlimited servings per container

Serving size　　　　**Overflowing cups**

Amount per serving

Christcharacter

Consumption is a great source for the following:　　**% Daily Value***

Intaking the breath of life	100%
Becoming the house of His glory	100%
Living the FULL life	100%
Cleansing the palate of anxiety	100%
Experiencing the pursuit of God	100%
Feeling refreshed in His arms	100%

*The % Daily Value (DV) tells you how much a nutrient in a serving contributes to a daily diet. Feasting on His Presence every day is recommended for heavenly nutritional health.

DESSERT

Creative Writing (DIY Dessert)

Take a moment to sit and dine on your favorite Psalm. Now, get alone in the Lord's presence and write about how you feel and what you see. Write about His glory, love, and any other characteristics that come to mind. Write to your Beloved and then read what you wrote. Savor the dessert you just created with Him.

Reflection Questions

How do you worship? Are your thoughts consumed by Him during worship or are you thinking about others, time, or how you look? Be honest. This is just for you. How can you focus on Him completely during worship?

Read Exodus 40. How do you feel when you realize that the presence of God described in this passage now dwells in you? This awesome and fearsome God now inhabits you. Write down your thoughts

COFFEE TIME!

His Special Brew

There are many different brews of coffee in the world, but I want to share Jesus' Special Brew with you. Jesus has created a rich blend of blessings, favor, assurance, and love that are unique with each cup. He has dreams and visions just for you.

I pray that you allow the robust aroma of His Special Brew to fill you up as you breathe it in. Many people do not like the bitter aftertaste some coffee has, but with this brew, there is none. When you drink it, you will feel His full-bodied warmth surround you. You will be left feeling supernaturally refreshed and energized.

For those of you who feel like you can't start your day without your cup of coffee, I challenge you to crave His Special Brew in the same way!

> Never doubt God's mighty power to work in you and accomplish all this. He will achieve infinitely more than your greatest request, your most unbelievable dream, and exceed your wildest imagination! He will outdo them all, for his miraculous power *constantly energizes you.*
>
> Ephesians 3:20 (TPT, italics added for emphasis)

DAY 9

FEAST ON HIS INTIMACY

Food for Thought: You can tell how rich your food is by how much it makes your heart burn.

For my old identity has been *co-crucified with Christ* and no longer lives. And now the essence of this new life is no longer mine, for the Anointed One lives his life through me—*we live in union as one*! My new life is empowered by the faith of the Son of God who loves me so much that he gave himself for me, dispensing his life into mine!

Galatians 2:20 (TPT, italics added for emphasis)

Union

Union is often defined as two separate things combining to become one new thing. Once you believe in Jesus, He takes you and combines you with Himself to create one new life *with* you! "You are living a brand-new kind of life that is continually learning more and more of what is right, and trying constantly to be more and more like Christ who created this new life within you" (Colossians 3:10, TLB).

At the end of yesterday's main course, I mentioned how the Lord was tired of having a barrier (veil) between you and Him. He wanted union with you. So how did He get this inseparable union? He took you to the cross with Him. As He took those nails into His flesh, so did you. But you felt no pain because He took it all. When He died, you died (Romans 6:6). When He was buried, you were buried (Romans 6:4). Here is the amazing part. When He rose from the dead, He raised a new you to life! This new you is one with Him. "For if we have become one with Him by sharing a death like His, we shall also be [one with Him in sharing] His resurrection [by a new life lived for God]" (Romans 6:5, AMPC, italics added for emphasis).

This new life does not include you carrying your old self. The old, broken, corrupted you stays dead and buried. There is no room in this union for the old, dead you. It doesn't exist anymore; Christ exists within you. He fills you up (Colossians 2:10). He hides you away with Him (Colossians 3:3). The intimacy you have with Him is not founded on what you can do for Him. It is about what you do with Him. His life in you cannot be destroyed or corrupted by your old self because you were born again when He raised you to life. "For you have been born again not of seed which is perishable, but imperishable, that is, through the living and enduring word of God" (1 Peter 1:23, NASB).

Christ is that living Word of God. That seed Christ planted in you is imperishable! Other translations say incorruptible (KJV). Christ in you makes you incorruptible! Now that we are incorruptible, Christ can take us by the hand, pull us out of the grave, and seat us with Him in heaven.

> But God is so rich in mercy and loves us with such intense love that, even when we were dead because of our acts of disobedience, he brought us to life along with the Messiah—it is by grace that you have been delivered. That is, God raised us up with the Messiah Yeshua and seated us with him in heaven.
>
> Ephesians 2:4-6 (CJB)

Before the beginning of time, God wanted union with us. He created this amazing love story throughout His Word to show us how much He wanted us. Feast on that intimacy with Him. Spend time doing stuff with

Him, not just for Him. Union is two becoming one. All it takes to live in union is to see the One in you.

The Bride

A few years ago, I was sitting at the Lord's table and thoughts on being crucified with Christ were slowly cooking in my mind. I then started to imagine what it would be like, and I wrote the following. I hope that as you read it, you will savor His intimacy.

> *There I was matted and ugly, full of fear. I was bound to my sin and filth, living in despair, and awaiting my judgement. Suddenly, a hand overshadowed mine. A nail pressed against my skin, driving through our hands together, but there was no pain. I saw His eyes staring deeply into mine with nothing but thoughts of love. As He let out His last breath, mine, too, was taken. Down to the grave we descended as I laid completely unbound from my sin. "It is finished," He whispered in my ear. "I have longed for this day for so long." I sat up and watched as my grave clothes turned into a shroud of glory. He took my hand, and we stepped out of the grave. I turned and saw the remnant of my old life lying there, covered in my old clothes. All my filth, sin, and decay were forever cut off from who I am now. He gently turned my face toward His, smiled, and guided me out of death once and for all. "Now we are one, my Bride."*

Jesus wants to take you into deeper intimacy. There is no great effort on your part. All you have to do is say "yes" to Him. It's like when you get married, all you do is say "yes" or "I do" and you are married. Marriage to the Bridegroom is union. He always wants more of you. He can't get enough of you. He doesn't need space away from you or alone time. He just wants you. He died for you. When we spend time with Him, we get transformed. It's a by-product. If you dine on the Beloved, you become more like the Beloved because you are taking Him into yourself. He starts to flow through your veins. I don't know about you, but it makes me so glad that He is an all-you-can-eat meal.

LET'S DRINK SOME COCO!

The prefix "Co" in Greek is [4]*syn* (G4862 pronounced "soon"). It is a primary preposition that represents union but a *much closer union* than *meta* (G3326) and *para* (G3844), which are often translated as the word "with." Wow! This word "co" means that we are in closer union than even the word "with" can convey!

What does this mean for us? Imagine that you are "with" someone. You might see yourself standing next to them or near them. Now imagine that you are "co" with someone. You are so close to that person, there is no space for anything to come between you! That is what Paul was trying to convey when he described himself as crucified, buried, raised, and seated with Christ. Paul used this word: *syn* (Co).

I am so grateful to Winnie *Cóco* Banov for sharing her "co" revelation from the Bible.

4   Thayer's Greek Lexicon

Intimacy Nutrition Label

Nutrition Facts

Unlimited servings per container

Serving size   **Overflowing cups**

Amount per serving

Christer

Christ

Consumption is a great source for the following: **% Daily Value***

Living life in union with Jesus	100%
Leaving the old you in the grave	100%
Becoming incorruptible	100%
Removing the toxins from the past	100%
Hearing your Beloved's voice	100%
Being transformed by drinking coco	100%

*The % Daily Value (DV) tells you how much a nutrient in a serving contributes to a daily diet. Feasting on His Intimacy every day is recommended for heavenly nutritional health.

DESSERT

A Divine Love Story

Today's dessert is like a serenade. I want you to drink in the love Jesus has for you as you read Song of Songs (Solomon). This book is like a depiction of Jesus and His Bride (you/the church). Read through this book in the Bible and see yourself as the Bride (Shulamite). I recommend reading it in different translations. I will post an excerpt from The Passion Translation here from Chapter 1, verses 2-4a:

The Shulamite

Let him smother me with kisses—his Spirit-kiss divine. So kind are your caresses, I drink them in like the sweetest wine! Your presence releases a fragrance so pleasing—over and over poured out. For your lovely name is 'Flowing Oil.' No wonder the brides-to-be adore you. Draw me into your heart. We will run away together into the king's cloud-filled chamber.

Reflection Questions

How do you spend intimate time with the Lord? Remember intimate time means being in close proximity.

After drinking some "Coco," how would you describe what it means to be co-crucified, co-buried, co-raised, and co-seated with Christ?

DAY 10

FEAST ON HIS RIGHTEOUSNESS

Food for Thought: Avoid feasting on junk food. It may look good, but it holds no real value.

He orchestrated this: the Anointed One, who had never experienced sin, *became sin* for us so that in Him *we might embody the very righteousness of God.*

2 Corinthians 5:21 (VOICE, italics added for emphasis)

What is Righteousness?

Read the verse at the top again. Because of Jesus, you embody the very righteousness of God! Chew on that for a while. Let it sink into your being. Let this fill you with supernatural nutrients. I did not always understand that Christ is the source of my righteousness with God. I grew up in church, hearing all about righteousness. I heard all the time how we needed to be righteous before God, but I don't remember anyone ever telling me what righteousness entails. Is it avoiding everything that looks like sin? Is it reading and praying for so many hours? How and when does God consider us righteous? As my hunger grew for more understanding, I started to dig into His Word. I learned what the word *righ-*

teousness means in the Greek. Let me share some of the morsels I found (italics are added to definitions for emphasis).

Righteousness ([5]*dikaiosynē*): the *character* or *quality* of being right or just.

1). It denotes an attribute of God.

2c). The sum total of requirements of God.

3a). Whereby all who believe on the Lord Jesus Christ are brought into *right relationship with God.*

3b). This righteousness is *unattainable by obedience to any law,* or by any merit of man's own, or any other condition than that of faith in Christ.

3c). The man who trusts in Christ *becomes the righteousness* of God in Him, i.e., becomes in Christ all that God requires of a man to be, all that he could never be himself.

The more I learned about righteousness, the more I understood that Christ is the answer to all the questions I had. I can't become righteous on my own or through performance. God already considers me righteous because of Christ in me! Christ fulfilled the requirements of God necessary for right standing before Him. I become righteous through Christ's righteousness!

> Yes, Adam's one sin brings condemnation for everyone, but Christ's one act of righteousness brings a right relationship with God and new life for everyone. Because one person disobeyed God, many became sinners. But because one other person obeyed God, many will be made righteous.
>
> Romans 5:18-19 (NLT)

I used to feel like I was in a pressure cooker, waiting for judgement to come because I thought righteousness required effort on my part. I felt like I was always messing up because I was always falling short of perfec-

---

5   Sourced from The New Strong's Expanded Exhaustive Concordance of the Bible Red Letter Ed. Italics added for emphasis (G1343)

tion. Now the pressure is off. Jesus' effort gives me what I need to stand pure before God.

Romans 10:4 says, "For Christ is the end of the law [it leads to Him and its purpose is fulfilled in Him], for [granting] righteousness to everyone who believes [in Him as Savior]" (AMP). Christ never falls short. He never misses the mark. It is through Him and His faithfulness that we receive the gift of righteousness. We just have to feast on His righteousness to see that He gave us His portion, and it is all we will ever need. "God's righteousness comes through the faithfulness of Jesus Christ for all who have faith in him. There's no distinction" (Romans 3:22, CEB). You have the righteousness of God because you believe in Jesus!

The Righteousness of a Holy King

Why is righteousness so important? God could not be in union with a sinful humanity. It goes against His nature, which is overflowing with holiness and glory. He longed to be close, to be intimate, but His nature is a force that opposes all that is sinful. A humanity steeped in sin would meet destruction if God tried to draw near to them with His presence. God's Son was the holy, spotless sacrifice that allotted us His virtue.

Without His righteousness, we as the Bride were unfit to be married to a Holy King. The union could never happen. That is why the King took off His royalty and died a lowly criminal's death, so that we could have a place in glory with Him. We have His righteousness now. When we feast on Him, we are inseparably connected with Him in body, mind, and spirit. His righteousness in us has finally made it possible for the Holy King to have full communion and union with a now spotless Bride.

The Righteous Life

Now that we understand that we are already granted the righteousness of God through Jesus, how does this affect our life? We start living our lives knowing that we have access to God now! We can stand before Him without fear or worry that we will never measure up. God no longer sees you as unworthy to stand in His presence. You can live a life knowing that you are not only right with God, but that you have qualities of Him inside you! You have *His* righteousness. When you look in the mirror, you can be proud of what you see because Jesus made you right. He makes you blameless.

I said this during an earlier meal, but when you know you are free, you can set others free. A righteous life is not constantly trying to earn a good standing with God, then becoming self-focused when we fall short. If we could earn righteousness, then Christ died for nothing (Galatians 2:21). A righteous life is lived when you know you already exist in good standing with God, can freely access everything in heaven, and then give it freely away to everyone around you!

Righteousness Nutrition Label

Nutrition Facts

Unlimited servings per container

Serving size   **Overflowing cups**

Amount per serving

Christ

Consumption is a great source

for the following: **% Daily Value***

Understanding righteousness	100%
Standing in right relationship with God	100%
Becoming all that God requires of you	100%
A palate change favoring Lamb	100%
Living in union with the Holy King	100%
Getting out of a pressure cooker	100%

*The % Daily Value (DV) tells you how much a nutrient in a serving contributes to a daily diet. Feasting on His Righteousness every day is recommended for heavenly nutritional health.

DESSERT

Spread the Good News Butter

I want you to find 2-3 people either in person or through technology and share what Christ has done for you. This is like a testimony time. Post it on social media, text someone, do something to spread the good news butter around. People want to be encouraged, and you are an encourager!

In the Throne Room

I want you to imagine that you are standing before God. He sees you in all that you are through Jesus. How do you feel? Now imagine that God is walking towards you, wrapping His arms around you, and embracing you. He turns to whisper in your ear. What does He say to you? Write it down.

Reflection Questions

What does it mean to "embody the very righteousness of God"? Read the verse of the day. Write down what that means about your identity.

Read Romans 3:22 again.
What does this verse mean to you?

DAY 11

FEAST ON HIS SPIRIT

Food for Thought: From which spirit is your fruit being produced?

> But you are not carnal but spiritual if the Spirit of God finds a home within you. You cannot, indeed, be a Christian at all unless you have something of his Spirit in you. Now if Christ does live within you his presence means that your sinful nature is dead, but your spirit becomes alive because of the righteousness he brings with him. I said that our nature is "dead" in the presence of Christ, and so it is, because of its sin. Nevertheless once the Spirit of him who raised Jesus from the dead lives within you he will, by that same Spirit, bring to your whole being new strength and vitality.
>
> Romans 8:9-11 (PHILLIPS)

The Empowerment of His Spirit

Today's feast is savoring the Holy Spirit, which includes multiple courses. This is a long feast so please feel free to take two days to fully finish this meal if necessary. It is hard to feast on His Spirit if we don't know all that His Spirit offers, so let's briefly look at who the Spirit is.

The Holy Spirit is the Helper that Jesus promised us when He returned to the right hand of the Father. He sent the Spirit so that we could constantly learn more about His ways (John 14:26). The Holy Spirit is God pouring out His Spirit upon all of us who believe in Jesus (Acts 2:17). This means that God gives us a part of Himself to empower us! It is the Lord's Spirit that changes us. It is that Spirit which gives us the ability to live a new life free from the shackles of sin. It is His Spirit that constantly renews us with supernatural vitality and strength! Now that we have the Holy Spirit, we are no longer alone or left by ourselves to struggle through life.

"Don't you realize that your body is the temple of the Holy Spirit, who lives in you and was given to you by God? You do not belong to yourself" (1 Corinthians 6:19, NLT). His Spirit has claimed us for His own! It's like when two people get married. They claim each other for themselves. They are bound to each other in a holy union to walk through life together. You belong to the Lord! He has claimed you for Himself with evidence of His Holy Spirit. He will never leave you or forsake you (Hebrews 13:5). Jesus made a vow with you when you said "yes" to Him. This vow includes His Spirit coming and empowering you. "But you will receive power when the Holy Spirit has come upon you; and you shall be My witnesses both in Jerusalem and in all Judea, and Samaria, and as far as the remotest part of the earth" (Acts 1:8, NASB). The Lord's Spirit is now fused with you and empowers you. What does this fusion look like? What does it include? Let's dig into our next course to find out.

Organic Fruit

But the fruit of the Spirit [the result of His presence within us] is love [unselfish concern for others], joy, [inner] peace, patience [not the ability to wait, but how we act while waiting], kindness, goodness, faithfulness, gentleness, self-control. Against such things there is no law.

Galatians 5:22-23 (AMP)

I hope you like fruit because we are now going to taste His fruit. Organic fruit is not manufactured in a production line or treated with synthetics. It is fruit that grows naturally and would still grow without human assistance and effort. The fruits of the Spirit are organic. They are not produced from self-effort or fruit management programs. They are produced by *the* Vine. Jesus is the Vine, and we are the branches (John 15:5). The Holy Spirit is what connects the branches to the Vine. It is what supplies the nutrients to each branch.

The fruits of the Spirit showcase all the attributes of Jesus. Jesus *is* love, He *is* joy, He *is* peace. As we partake in His Spirit, we start producing His fruit. Our union to the Vine is so close that we can't help but produce His fruit. We don't strive to manufacture fruit. It's completely organic. We just simply feast on the nutrients that the Vine supplies, and they naturally grow in and through us. The fruit of His Spirit is not based on circumstances or fleeting emotions, it is based on union with the Vine. The more you stay connected to the Vine, the more fruit grows on you.

Holy Spirit Spice Rack

Now that we have tasted some fruit, let's get into some spices. Imagine that the Holy Spirit is like a full spice rack. Each spice is a gift that will bring a special flavor to your life. If you have ever cooked with strong spices, you know that there is evidence of them in the meal. There is a distinct smell, flavor, and sometimes texture. The gifts of the Holy Spirit are the same. If you have the Holy Spirit, there should be evidence in your life. You should be filled with Holy Spirit seasonings!

For too long, the world has tasted a bland version of the gospel. They have heard the gospel, but have they seen it demonstrated? Jesus told us that we are supposed to be the salt of the earth; we cannot lose our flavor, otherwise we are not good for anything (Matthew 5:13). The gifts of the Holy Spirit, these spices, are how the world sees the gospel in action. Jesus didn't just preach the kingdom of heaven, He showcased it. Even

Paul told us that his message was not with persuasive words but with demonstrations of the Spirit and of power (1 Corinthians 2:4).

I want to spend some time during this meal looking at the amazing seasonings offered by the Holy Spirit. In 1 Corinthians 12, Paul talks about the gifts of the Spirit and how God gives these distinct spiritual gifts through His one Spirit (1 Corinthians 12:4-11). Are you ready to marinate in His seasonings so much that you look, smell, and become different? Are you ready to show the world what a perfectly seasoned gospel tastes like? The Holy Spirit is ready to spice up your life with all His supernatural gifts. Let's look at each spice and just spend time absorbing all the flavors.

Word of Wisdom: Revelation and insight given by God, often for the purpose of solving problems or complex situations. God-given supernatural solutions that were formerly unclear or unseen.

We will taste more of the Lord's wisdom on Day 25, but today I want to mention that all throughout the Bible, seeking the Lord's wisdom is a repeated theme. The world needs heaven's wisdom. It needs solutions to problems that are eternal and provide true prosperity and freedom. Human wisdom can only go so far, but God's wisdom is beyond measure. You have access to this divine wisdom through the Holy Spirit. Ask for supernatural solutions for your workplace, your family, and your friends. They need the wisdom of God in their finances, relationships, and daily life. The Holy Spirit is your source for this wisdom, and He is so faithful to provide.

Word of Knowledge: Revelation and knowledge given by God, containing facts that relate to the past or present in someone's life. God-given supernatural information that cannot be known by oneself, which is to demonstrate His goodness.

I love this gift because words of knowledge are an extraordinary way God opens people's hearts to notice Him. Let me share a testimony with you. One day, I was sitting with the Lord, asking Him for words of knowledge about people before going out on a treasure hunt (I recommend Kevin Dedman's, *The Ultimate Treasure Hunt: A Guide to Supernatural Evangelism Through Supernatural Encounters)*. The Lord gave me some very odd words, and I wrote them down because I knew they would lead me to the person He wanted me to find. I wrote down the following: *Location: art gallery, or art in windows. Appearance: Big jewels, arrows. Name: Judy. Healing Needs: Family relationships.*

I took my treasure map, and we went to a strip mall that had multiple stores. I started walking and encouraging people as I met them. Suddenly, one of the other ladies in my group came to me excited because she saw some artwork inside a boutique shop. She knew I had art on my map, so we went into the store. There was this beautiful lady right in front of me, wearing these big red jewels. I was immediately super excited. I knew she was my treasure! I went up to her and asked her for her name. She told me her name was Judy. I started laughing because, of course, God would bring me to Judy.

I pulled out my map with all the words of knowledge that the Spirit had spoken to me earlier and showed her. She was amazed. She couldn't believe that even her name was there. I told her that she was the treasure that God had led me to, and I started prophesying over her. My friend was standing behind her and motioned to me to look at Judy's hair pin. She was wearing a hairpin shaped like arrows! Another wave of joy went through the shop. I then asked her about her family. By now Judy was just marveling at how much God saw her and wanted to lavish His love on her.

She told me that she had some broken relationships with her family. I pointed to the part of my map that had *healing relationships* written down, so she knew God was going to do something. I started to pray for healing over her family. Judy turned to me and told me that day was her first day on the job, that she wasn't even supposed to start working there until the next day! She couldn't believe that God had orchestrated this divine appointment just for her. God was able to touch Judy's life that day because I sat with Him and asked Him to share His knowledge with me. You too can ask the Lord for words of knowledge to see healings and breakthroughs happen in people's lives. One very important thing to remember, though, is that you have to do something with the knowledge He shares.

The Gift of Faith: The supernatural ability to believe God without human doubt, unbelief, or reasonings. Doubt cannot exist when this gift is stirred up.

Have you ever experienced a situation where you knew that God was going to do what you needed Him to do? In that situation, you could not even imagine God not doing it. It was like faith enveloped you and nothing outside of faith existed. This is what the gift of faith is like.

Let me share a testimony. I was in a cliff-diving accident in Japan which tore the ligaments in both my knees. I couldn't walk, was put into a cast, and even had to use a wheelchair for a while. I was supposed to take my students mountain climbing in a couple of weeks. Everyone told me there was no way I could climb a mountain with my knees messed up like they were. The gift of faith rose within me. I knew that I was going mountain climbing with my students. I didn't care what the doctors said or what the x-rays showed; I was going.

Right before I was supposed to have my knee surgery scheduled, I was with my husband and best friend, praying. The trip was in just a few days, and my knees were still messed up. I still had absolute faith even though most people around me were telling me it wasn't possible. While praying, the Lord told me to take the brace off and get on my knees. After arguing internally for a split second, I did. I took off my brace and got on my knees. My knees had not been moved or bent in weeks. I was immediately hit with extreme pain, but then I felt my knees catch on fire. All the pain left, and I felt Jesus knit my tendons back together. I felt my knees become whole again.

It is so hard to explain that feeling with words. I got off the floor and started running and jumping around the room. No pain. My knees were completely healed! A few days later, I stood on top of that mountain and testified to my students about the goodness of God and how He heals. The gift of faith is unstoppable, unmovable, and unrelenting. It is a spice that doesn't just change you, but also those around you.

Healing: Supernatural power that heals all sickness, diseases, and afflictions in all areas of the body—physical, mental, and emotional.

Jesus loves to heal, and He wants us to continue His work now. His Spirit in us is how we see healing happen. There is nothing that cannot be healed, and the closer we get to Jesus, the more we see Him heal through us. If you long to see more healing in your life, remember to sit at His table and dine with Him. Feast on His heart of healing compassion. He is the source of all healing, so partner with Him and let Him use you to do His will on this earth. The more people you pray with for healing, the more people you will see receive healing. If you do not pray for the sick, how can you see the sick healed? I encourage you to go back to Day 5 and feast on His healing again!

Working of Miracles: A supernatural power to interfere in the ways of nature that can counteract natural law if God decides. Examples: walking on water, calming storms, and raising the dead.

When I was little, I used to be amazed while reading the Bible and hearing the stories of how God parted the Red Sea for Moses, how three men were thrown into a fiery furnace only to walk out without even smelling like smoke, and how Jesus multiplied food to feed thousands of people. These are signs and wonders.

Let me share a testimony of one of the times I encountered a miracle. I was around 10 years old, and it was wintertime. I lived next to a lake, and my friend and I were playing near it. My friend's younger sister, who was very small and light, started walking on the lake. We told her to stop because we knew the lake only had a thin layer of ice. However, she kept walking further out onto the lake. The ice broke, and she fell in. I immediately ran toward the lake and realized that I was a lot bigger and heavier than her, so I would certainly fall in if I tried to walk on the ice. Suddenly, the story of Jesus walking on water came to my mind, and I just started walking on the ice. I got all the way to that hole, lifted her out of the water, and carried her back to shore.

There is no way in the natural order of things that the ice didn't break for me. I was even heavier walking back to shore since I was carrying her back with me. It was a miracle that defied logic and reasoning. I had walked on something that I should not have been able to walk on. Every time I recall this testimony, I smile because Jesus wants to give us what we ask for to show the world His goodness. The Holy Spirit allows us to operate in signs and wonders if we just ask and believe. *All* things are possible to those who believe (Mark 9:23).

Prophecy: A divine message given in a known language. A prophetic message is not formed by human thought but instead given by God for the purpose of edification, comfort, and exhortation.

I find it interesting how Paul wrote that we should earnestly desire all the gifts, but especially to prophesy (1 Corinthians 14:1). Why is prophecy so important? The simple answer is because it is how God wants to communicate to people their value to Him.

When we prophesy, we are giving God access to use us as messengers for His love letters to those around us. Prophetic words are supposed to be for edification, comfort, and exhortation. God wants everyone to know how much He loves them, and how much He cares about their daily lives and circumstances. He wants people to know that He sees them.

Let me share a testimony from my husband. During Christmastime he was asked to pray and give prophetic words to a few people in a ministry group. He prayed for those people and asked God for a prophetic word. For one lady, God showed him an image of a fur lined coat. He then asked the Lord what this image meant for this lady. The coat represented a covering that God had made just for her. It was tailor-made for her ministry and life. No matter where she went or what she did, her covering would keep her safe, warm, and effective. Later, this lady testified to the impact of this prophetic word. She said that she was going through a tough time and doubting her effectiveness and impact on the people around her. This word spoke directly to her, and God encouraged her that He has already provided her with a complete covering that can never be ruined by mistakes or supposed failures.

Prophecy can lift people out of the mud and help them see their identity in Christ. For too long, the Enemy has taken away the power of prophecy by convincing us that only a select chosen are anointed to operate in this gift. I grew up thinking that only "the anointed" could prophesy. I believed that God only gave a few people access to the spiritual gifts. I didn't understand until I started feasting in His Word that we should desire all the gifts that Jesus has provided.

Once I understood that I also have access to the gift of prophecy, I started flexing my prophetic muscle. I started to listen to the Lord for His words. I started to learn how to recognize His voice instead of my own. I started to be bold and release what the Lord wanted me to release. I love asking the Lord for words that will uplift people around me, whether I'm in the grocery store, church, work, or with family. We all have access to this amazing gift. The more you step out in prophecy, the more you will see how awesome it is to demonstrate how much Jesus loves the world!

Discernment of Spirits: Revelation and insight given by God to understand if there are spirits present and what their plans might be.

I like to think of this gift as being a spiritual bouncer. Bouncers are people who keep watch and notice when things are about to be disrupted in a negative way. Bouncers are also the ones who remove the disruptions and keep the peace. The gift of discernment allows us to see what is going on behind the scenes in the spirit realm. Without the gift of discernment, the Enemy can infiltrate the church and ministries to wreak havoc. Without the gift of discernment, no one would recognize disruptions as the Enemy or learn what his plans are.

God wants all of us to be able to discern His plans and the Enemy's plans. He wants His people to recognize when it is Him moving or when it is a distraction from Satan. This gift needs to be strongly connected to wisdom, especially when dealing with people. Pay attention when an alarm bell goes off inside you. I met a guy once on a trip with my friends. He was very friendly on the outside, but I was seeing "Red Alert" all around me. This man started paying attention to my friend. I told my friend to be careful with this guy and not go anywhere alone with him. She came to me later and said that he tried to get her alone and when she said "no," he tried to force her. She ended up running away.

Thank Jesus that He gives us warnings to pray and help others to not fall into the Enemy's plans. Ask the Lord: is this person being authentic or making a show to disrupt others? Does what I'm hearing align with the Word of God or result in false doctrine? The Holy Spirit is the discerner in you; ask Him and He will guide you.

Various Kinds of Tongues: The supernatural ability to speak in divine utterances that are not in the speaker's known language.

I like to consider this a two-fold spice. Part of the gift of speaking in tongues is used during a corporate gathering. The Lord will give a message to the corporate body using an unknown tongue. This must be followed by an interpretation if it is to be fruitful to the body (1 Corinthians 14:6-17). There is so much power to edify the church when tongues are corporately released, followed by the interpretation.

Another part of speaking in tongues is for our own edification (1 Corinthians 14:4). When we speak in tongues without interpretation, we edify ourselves because our spirit is speaking directly to God. "For he who speaks in a tongue does not speak to men but to God, for no one understands him; however, in the spirit he speaks mysteries" (1 Corinthians 14:2, NKJV). Praying in tongues is a wonderful way to pray for those around us when we cannot find the words to pray on our own.

When my mom told me of her breast cancer diagnosis, I didn't know what to pray, but the Spirit is so faithful to pray for me. "And the Holy Spirit helps us in our weakness. For example, we don't know what God wants us to pray for. But the Holy Spirit prays for us with groanings that cannot be expressed in words" (Romans 8:26, NLT). I prayed in tongues a lot for my mom. I knew that the Holy Spirit in me could express what I didn't have the words to say. I always feel so empowered when I pray in tongues because it feels like I'm connecting my spirit with His Spirit.

However, when I'm praying for others aloud, I pray in English because what good does it do them when they cannot connect or agree with what I'm saying? Paul stressed this in his letter to the Corinthians: speaking in tongues is great for self-edification, but it needs to be interpreted if it is to edify another.

Interpretation of Tongues: The supernatural ability to interpret in the native language when a divine utterance is given. In many cases, the interpreter does not know the language of the divine utterance.

I love seeing people operate in this gift. When God gives us a message through tongues, there is a sweet reverence that comes along with the interpretation. Everyone gets quiet, in awe of hearing all that the Lord has to say. I remember when I was flooded with this gift during a church service. Someone started speaking in tongues in front of the entire congregation and everything got quiet. When the person speaking in tongues stopped, there was a hush to see what would happen next. I had never operated in this gift, so I had no idea what it would be like. It was like my whole body was suddenly taken over by the Holy Spirit. My mouth opened and words came out. I was able to register what I was saying, but it was with an authority I had never known before. I felt like power was imbued in the words coming out of my mouth. After the Spirit was done interpreting, I was overwhelmed by His glory and just sat down in awe of Him. I realized how much He loves talking with His people, how He loved sharing His heart for us at that specific moment. It is always amazing to see this gift.

Aroma of Heaven

Sometimes it is good to be reminded of who lives in you, who produces the fruit, and who flavors your life. You are directly connected to the Vine. You have *the* Spirit of Jesus living and breathing within you! "And when He had said this, He breathed on them and said to them, 'Receive the Holy Spirit'" (John 20:22, NASB).

The very breath of the Lord is in you! Through His Spirit you have access to the mind of Christ. This allows us to think like Him and speak like Him. His Spirit changes your thought processes and helps you to unravel some of the mysteries and revelations of God. The Holy Spirit is who gives you access to unlimited resources. Sit and rest in His Spirit, and your life will never look, feel, or taste the same. You will carry an aroma of heaven with you wherever you go.

Holy Spirit Nutrition Label

Nutrition Facts

Unlimited servings per container

Serving size   **Overflowing cups**

Amount per serving

Christh

Consumption is a great source for the following: % Daily Value*

Producing organic fruit	100%
Living an empowered life	100%
Demonstrating a flavorful gospel	100%
Releasing the aroma of heaven	100%
Staying directly connected to the Vine	100%
Getting away from *man*ufactured fruit	100%

*The % Daily Value (DV) tells you how much a nutrient in a serving contributes to a daily diet. Feasting on His Spirit every day is recommended for heavenly nutritional health.

DESSERT

The Spice is Right

I want you to sit at the Lord's table and put His spices into action. Let's do three spicy activations:

- *Prophecy*—Appearance: Find someone and ask the Lord for a word for that person based on something they are wearing. Remember, the word should be to encourage, edify, and/or comfort.
- *Word of Knowledge*—Ask the Lord to give you some healing words of knowledge for people you will encounter this week. It could be for a family member, co-worker, classmate, etc. The word could be something simple, such as hearing or seeing the word "tinnitus." It could be more detailed like seeing/hearing someone has nerve pain in the left side of their neck due to a recent car accident. Release the word of knowledge God gave you by sharing it with the person He directs you to.
- *Discernment*—Ask the Lord to help you discern what kind of spirit is producing fruit in your life. This could include paying attention to the words coming out of your mouth. Are your words often negative, angry, bitter, happy, or uplifting? This could also include how you react when negative situations happen.

Reflection Questions

Which fruits of the Spirit are evident in your life? List three pieces of evidence.

Which gift of the Holy Spirit do you want to grow in? How do you plan to grow in it?

Remember, we can always ask God to increase these gifts by praying, believing, and receiving (Mark 11:24)!

DAY 12

FEAST ON HIS BREAD

Food for Thought: Jesus is your Bread. Get to know the Baker.

I am the *living bread* that came down from heaven. Anyone who eats this bread will live forever; and this bread, which I will offer so the world may live, is my flesh.

John 6:51 (NLT, italics added for emphasis)

The Bread of Life

Today I want to start the meal by reading a few verses from John 6. I want you to savor these verses as you read. Chew on the parts that might be difficult to understand. Jesus said these words for a reason, and we need to feast on them so that we might get a deeper revelation from them.

"I am the living bread that came down from heaven. Anyone who eats this bread will live forever; and this bread, which I will offer so the world may live, is my flesh." [52] Then the people began arguing with each other about what he meant. "How can this man give us his flesh to eat?" they asked. [53] So Jesus said again, "I tell you the truth, unless you eat the flesh of the Son of Man and drink his blood, you cannot have eternal life within you. [54] But anyone who eats my flesh and drinks my blood has eternal life, and I will raise that person at the last day. ⁵⁵ For *my flesh is true food,* and *my blood is true drink.* ⁵⁶ Anyone who eats my flesh and drinks my blood remains in me, and I in him. ⁵⁷ I live because of the living Father who sent me; in the same way, anyone who feeds on me will live because of me."

John 6:51-57 (NLT, italics added for emphasis).

I grew up reading these verses, and I always had questions. Why would Jesus tell people to eat His flesh and drink His blood when He knew eating human flesh and drinking blood were taboo to the Jews? Why did Jesus describe Himself as bread? Many disciples deserted Jesus after this because they were offended by what He said (John 6:61-66).

Jesus wanted the people to know that He came as bread from heaven to satisfy a spiritual hunger. In order to be spiritually satisfied, you have to consume the Bread of Life. You can't just know about Him or watch Him do miracles; you must take Him inside of you because He is complete sustenance.

Bread was a source of life during Jesus' day. The grain and the bread made from it were the main staples of nourishment. Bread represented provision and often all food. Many times, bread would be the only food. Jesus described Himself as bread because He wanted people to understand that He is *the* source of *eternal* life! He is *the* source of provision and the only way to experience complete fulfilment. When we eat natural bread, our body absorbs the nutrients from it. The nutrients then provide our bodies with the different components needed to live. It is the same with the Bread of Life. When we feast on His Bread, we absorb Him and His Spirit. This Spirit then goes on to provide our bodies with everything needed for eternal life.

It is interesting to note that at the beginning of John chapter 6, Jesus feeds thousands of people with five loaves of bread and two fish (verses 1-15). The crowd witnessed Him producing physical bread to satisfy their physical hunger, but they could not understand when He related Himself as the Bread of Life to free them from spiritual malnourishment. "The true bread of God is the one who comes down from heaven and gives life to the world" (John 6:33, NLT). Jesus continued to say, "I am the bread of life. Whoever comes to me will never be hungry again. Whoever believes in me will never be thirsty" (John 6:35, NLT). Jesus was trying to tell the people that there was now access to a supernatural bread that would forever satisfy them. Have you eaten the Bread of Life who satisfies all hunger?

True Food

Adam and Eve ate some [6]food they weren't supposed to eat. Consuming this food opened an insatiable void in humanity. When the Israelites were in the wilderness, God provided manna from heaven, but it would only temporarily satisfy. When God sent Jesus, He sent Him to be true food (John 6:55).

True food remains after it is consumed. It flows throughout the body of the person who eats it. True food is not a temporary fix to get us through life. It is a permanent fix to finally satisfy the void created through Adam and Eve. Jesus is our true food. He is our eternal life! What transformation happens when you feast on this true food? You live in the revelation of His Word. You have His faith. You share His compassion. You see Him heal through you. All this and more are what happens when you feast on Him. You become enhanced. You receive His Spirt. His Word is planted inside of you.

As the "Word made flesh", feasting on Jesus means to take in all His Word and absorb it into our entire being. This is another step toward dwelling in Him as He dwells in us (1 John 4:13-15). We let the One who sustains us become our source of life—our source of everything. We become beacons of the Spirit and power because we have consumed

---

6   Tree of Knowledge of Good and Evil

all of Him as our sustenance. As we learned during our meal on Day 6, when feasting on His Word, we can't just understand the Word, we must believe it. We must live it.

As we feast on Jesus, His body, this Bread of Life, we are filled with Him beyond measure. Jesus is the heart of God, and by eating Him, we draw closer to God. We understand more of God's heart and His thoughts toward us. As we eat Jesus' body, we consume His Spirit, and it remains in us. Jesus tells us that anyone who feeds on Him will live forever. I grew up hearing people say, "We are what we eat." I don't know about you, but I want to be just like Jesus. If that saying is true, the more I consume Him, the more I become like Him.

Bread Nutrition Label

Nutrition Facts

Unlimited servings per container

Serving size   **Overflowing cups**

Amount per serving

Christist

Consumption is a great source

for the following: **% Daily Value***

Eternal Life	100%
Destroying spiritual malnourishment	100%
Getting every nutrient you need	100%
Absorbing supernatural life	100%
Being in the presence of the Baker	100%
Recognizing fake food when you see it	100%

*The % Daily Value (DV) tells you how much a nutrient in a serving contributes to a daily diet. Feasting on His Bread every day is recommended for heavenly nutritional health.

DESSERT

Bread of the Presence

In Exodus 25:30, the Word tells us that the Bread of the Presence was to always remain on the table before God. The Bread of the Presence were 12 loaves of bread that represented the 12 tribes of Israel; they were a symbol of God's provision and nourishment (Leviticus 24). I want you to think about how this Bread of the Presence is now represented in Jesus. Get a piece of bread (a real one). Look at it as the Bread of Life, the Bread of *His* Presence. Hold it in your hand. Let the reality of all that this Bread means sink into you. Now eat it! Let this Bread be absorbed into your mind, your spirit, and your body. Write down what you are feeling. Write down any revelations you received when you ate the Bread.

Reflection Questions

What are your thoughts when you read about Jesus telling the people to eat His flesh and drink His blood? What does this mean to you now?

I used to play a game called *Super Mario Brothers.* When Mario, the main character, punched these special question mark boxes, he would consume a power up. Mario transformed based on what he ate. He would gain special abilities. When you eat true food, what happens to you?

DAY 13

FEAST ON HIS WINE

Food for Thought: The best wine can only come from the true Vine.

And he took a cup of wine and gave thanks to God for it. He gave it to them and said, "Each of you drink from it, for this is my blood, which confirms the covenant between God and his people. It is poured out as a sacrifice to forgive the sins of many."

Matthew 26:27-28 (NLT)

Drink Him In

Oh, how I have been looking forward to this feast! There is nothing like the blood of the Lamb. To me, this meal is like diving deeper into the feast we had on Day 2: *Feast on His Finished Work*. The blood is the beginning of everything for us. When Jesus shed His blood on the cross, He began your new life. Let's drink in the power of His blood.

His Blood Brings Life

Remember, Jesus said in John 6:53 that His blood is *true drink* and without it there is no life in us. Without His sacrifice, we could never truly live. Death cannot exist in heaven, and when we were dead in sin, we could not exist in heaven. The power of His blood breathed us back into existence with God. This is how we are seated next to Jesus (Ephesians 2:6).

The Word tells us that life is in the blood (Leviticus 17:11). Through the blood of Jesus, we receive eternal life because His blood creates a new life in us. His blood has the power to pierce our soul and recreate us from the inside out. Taste His true drink and you will never be satisfied with anything else.

His Blood Cleanses Us

Jesus' blood didn't just wash us off on the outside. His blood washed us from the inside out. His blood *made* us free from all the filth of sin and shame. It cleansed us.

> "But if we [really] walk in the Light [that is, live each and every day in conformity with the precepts of God], as He Himself is in the Light, we have [true, unbroken] fellowship with one another [He with us, and we with Him], and the blood of Jesus His Son cleanses us from all sin [by *erasing the stain of sin*, keeping us cleansed from sin in all its forms and manifestations]."
>
> 1 John 1:7 (AMP, italics added for emphasis)

His blood is holy. That means when His blood washes over you, it strips you of everything that made you unholy. You cannot sit at His table, feast on His blood, and see yourself as dirty. His blood made you clean from the inside out. Anyone who still claims to be dirty after being washed in His blood is deceived into believing that His blood was not powerful enough to make us clean. What is the truth? His holy blood erased every stain of sin from within you.

His Blood Reconciles Us

When Jesus spilled His blood for us, His blood declared us innocent. And with that declaration, we can be friends with God!

And since by his blood he did all this for us as sinners, how much more will he do for us now that he has declared us not guilty? Now he will save us from all of God's wrath to come. And since, when we were his enemies, we were brought back to God by the death of his Son, what blessings he must have for us now that we are his friends and he is living within us! Now we rejoice in our wonderful new relationship with God—all because of what our Lord Jesus Christ has done in dying for our sins—making us friends of God.

Romans 5:9-11 (TLB)

The blood of Jesus transformed our relationship with God from animosity into intimacy. We can now be God's friends! Friends share their hearts with each other; they like each other. Have you ever thought of yourself as God's friend? I hope so! He doesn't just love you; He likes you! No longer do we have to live in fear of God's wrath. We now live life in the joy of God's favor. By the blood of Jesus, we are reconciled once and for all! Drink that in!

His Blood Redeems Us

You are redeemed by the blood. "In him we have redemption through his blood, the forgiveness of our trespasses, according to the riches of his grace" (Ephesians 1:7, CSB). Imagine all the terrible things you have done being thrown upon Jesus. Addictions, rage, promiscuity, violent behavior, etc. As soon as it barely touches the blood, it all dissolves. Those things that corrupted you—that chained you—just disappeared. The blood saved you. The blood established you as His Bride.

It is time to stop living as though we are going through a redemption process. We already have redemption! His blood redeemed you when you touched Him. It is time to rejoice, for the Bride has been given back the authority to advance the Bridegroom's kingdom!

His Blood Heals Us

When Jesus took each sting of the whip, each beating, more blood poured out from Him. Each wound and lashing brought about the destruction of sickness and disease. With every drop of blood, sickness and decay lost its power. With each drop, we gained a victory. It is the power of Jesus' blood that healed back then, heals today, and will heal in days to come. Jesus shed so much blood for us to be whole.

When sickness tries to attach itself to me, I just drink in His true drink. I want Jesus to receive all that He paid for with His blood. That includes my health, my wholeness, and my abundant life. By His wounds, we were healed (1 Peter 2:24)! The truth is that there is no such thing as "incurable" in Jesus Christ.

His Blood Brings Peace

Colossians 1:19-20 says, "For God in all his fullness was pleased to live in Christ, and through him God reconciled everything to himself. He made peace with everything in heaven and on earth by means of Christ's blood on the cross" (NLT). Before the blood was shed, everything was at war because sin held everything in bondage. Even the world was in chaos due to sin. When Jesus' blood ran down that cross, it brought a supernatural peace with it. Jesus stripped sin of its power and created a gateway to the Holy of Holies. The world needs to see what His peace looks like. We have the power of His blood coursing through our veins and that blood brings peace everywhere it goes.

His Blood Brings a New Covenant to Us

> After supper he took another cup of wine and said, "This cup is the new covenant between God and his people—an agreement confirmed with my blood, which is poured out as a sacrifice for you."
>
> Luke 22:20 (NLT)

All throughout today's meal, we have been drinking in His blood. In Luke 22:20, you see Jesus establishing the new covenant, not just for the disciples but for all of us. His blood sealed the covenant and established a new decree with God. His sacrifice tore the veil between heaven and earth. Jesus' blood fulfilled everything required by God for us to be in union with Him. We can now be brought near to God and experience all the blessings of Him today.

Ephesians 2:13 says, "But now you have been united with Christ Jesus. Once you were far away from God, but now you have been brought near to him through the blood of Christ" (NLT). Jesus shed His blood and said, "It is finished." That new covenant was put into effect the moment Jesus freely gave up His life. This covenant is not based on our performance, but on His. Our participation comes through resting in Him, and drinking, and feasting. So, let's remember all He did for us as we pick up our cup and continually drink Him in.

Wine Nutrition Label

Nutrition Facts

Unlimited servings per container

Serving size   **Overflowing cups**

Amount per serving

Christ

Consumption is a great source for

the following: **% Daily Value***

Being washed from the inside out	100%
Experiencing endless life	100%
Seeing yourself as God's friend	100%
Living as the redeemed	100%
Bringing peace to the world	100%
Remembering all Jesus has done	100%

*The % Daily Value (DV) tells you how much a nutrient in a serving contributes to a daily diet. Feasting on His Wine every day is recommended for heavenly nutritional health.

DESSERT

The Lord's Supper

The Lord's Supper is when we take bread and a cup, representing the body and blood of Jesus, and eat it to remember all that He has done for us. I personally love to eat the Lord's Supper because it brings me great joy! I eat His body and drink His blood. I feast on all He finished for me, to me, and in me.

Yesterday, we took the bread. Today, I want you to go get a drink. We just feasted on the power of His blood. I want you to look at your drink and see all that power. See all that His blood accomplished. Then, drink it! Let His blood wash over you with waves of joy! Let yourself feel His peace, His love, and His redemption. Drink more if you need. Let it all sink into your core. Take a moment and write down what you experience.

Reflection Questions

Which aspect of His blood affected you the most today? Write down why it affected you.

What comes to your mind when you read Jesus' words about the new covenant? How could you share what life looks like under the new covenant?

DAILY BREAD SPECIALS

Eternal Life

served with a side of everything you could ever wish for

Mind Transformation

served with a side of freedom and joy for spreading

DAY 14

FEAST ON HIS PROMISES

Food for Thought: Is food just fuel, or does slowing down and savoring it change the experience?

For as many as the promises of God are, in Him they are yes; therefore through Him also is our Amen to the glory of God through us.

2 Corinthians 1:20 (NASB)

Promise: Expect the Fulfillment of His Word

There are so many promises in the Bible. While creating this meal plan, I did a lot of taste testing, and it was fabulous! There is so much to His promises, and they are for *you*! All of them! I encourage you to discover more of the Lord's promises after today's feast. His promises became a "yes" because of Jesus, and that is why we just say "amen" while we live them out in our lives. If you find yourself struggling with uncertainty in different areas of your life, relish His promises for that area.

Today's meal is a little different. I'm going to share with you a tiny portion of His promises with evidence from the Word. I want you to chew on them. These promises need to get into your heart, mind, and body. You can't just read them; you need to absorb them, believe them, and live them. I've said this before: when you eat food, the nutrients from that food are released into your body and become a part of you. Let His promises become a part of you.

Promise of Rest: "Come to me, all of you who are struggling and burdened, and I will give you rest" (Matthew 11:28, CJB).

Promise for Peace: "Peace is what I leave with you; it is my own peace that I give you. I do not give it as the world does. Do not be worried and upset; do not be afraid" (John 14:27, GNT).

Promise to Guide: "Trust God from the bottom of your heart; don't try to figure out everything on your own. Listen for God's voice in everything you do, everywhere you go; he's the one who will keep you on track" (Proverbs 3:5-6, MSG).

Promise to Accompany: "Be strong and courageous, do not be afraid or in dread of them, for the Lord your God is the One who is going with you. He will not desert you or abandon you" (Deuteronomy 31:6, NASB).

Promise to Provide: "So don't worry about these things, saying, 'What will we eat? What will we drink? What will we wear?' These things dominate the thoughts of unbelievers, but your heavenly Father already knows all your needs. Seek the Kingdom of God above all else, and live righteously, and he will give you everything you need" (Matthew 6:31-33, NLT).

Promise for Strength: "Do not fear, for I am with you; Do not be afraid, for I am your God. I will strengthen you, I will also help you, I will also uphold you with My righteous right hand" (Isaiah 41:10, NASB).

Promise for Healing: "He heals the brokenhearted and binds up their wounds [curing their pains and their sorrows]" (Psalm 147:3, AMPC).

"When sickness comes, the Eternal is beside them—to comfort them on their sickbeds and restore them to health" (Psalm 41:3, VOICE).

Promise of Restoration: "So I will restore to you the years that the swarming locust has eaten" (Joel 2:25a, NKJV).

Promise of Forgiveness: "I, yes, I alone am he who blots away your sins for my own sake and will never think of them again" (Isaiah 43:25, TLB).

Promise to Answer Prayer: "Therefore I tell you, whatever you ask in prayer, believe that you have received it, and it will be yours" (Mark 11:24, ESV).

Promise of Joy: "When you obey me you are living in my love, just as I obey my Father and live in his love. I have told you this so that you will be filled with my joy. Yes, your cup of joy will over-flow!" (John 15:10-11, TLB).

Promise for a New Spirit and a New Heart: "And I will give you a new heart, and I will put a new spirit in you. I will take out your stony, stubborn heart and give you a tender, responsive heart. And I will put my Spirit in you so that you will follow my decrees and be careful to obey my regulations" (Ezekiel 36:26-27, NLT).

Promise to Rescue: "The righteous person faces many troubles, but the LORD comes to the rescue each time" (Psalm 34:19, NLT).

Promise of a Sound Mind: "For God has not given us a spirit of fear, but of power and of love and of a sound mind" (2 Timothy 1:7, NKJV).

Promise of Superhuman Energy: "For this I labor [unto weariness], striving with all the superhuman energy which He so mightily enkindles and works within me" (Colossians 1:29, AMPC).

Promise to be Heirs: "For now that you have faith in Christ you are all sons of God. All of you who were baptised 'into' Christ have put on the family likeness of Christ. Gone is the distinction be-tween Jew and Greek, slave and free man, male and female—you are all one in Christ Jesus. And if you belong to Christ, you are true descendants of Abraham, you are true heirs of his promise" (Galatians 3:28-29, PHILLIPS).

Promise to Destroy Strongholds: "The weapons we use in our fight are not the world's weapons but God's powerful weapons, which we use to destroy strongholds. We destroy false arguments; we pull down every proud obstacle that is raised against the knowledge of God; we take every thought captive and make it obey Christ" (2 Corinthians 10:4-5, GNT).

Promise of Victory: "But thanks be to God, Who gives us the victory [making us conquerors] through our Lord Jesus Christ" (1 Corinthians 15:57, AMPC).

Promise of Abundance: "The Eternal will give you more than enough of every good thing—children, cattle, and crops—as you live on the ground He promised your ancestors He'd give you" (Deuteronomy 28:11, VOICE).

Promise of Eternal Life: "This is the promise which He Himself made to us: eternal life" (1 John 2:25, NASB).

To end this meal, we just simply sit back, relax, and let these promises digest in us. All His promises are "yes" and "amen."

Promises Nutrition Label

Nutrition Facts

Unlimited servings per container

Serving size   **Overflowing cups**

Amount per serving

Christd

Consumption is a great source for

the following: **% Daily Value***

Daily dose of peace	100%
Living in great expectation	100%
Seeing the power of the promise	100%
Being filled with superhuman energy	100%
Praying with expectation	100%
Knowing these promises belong to you	100%

*The % Daily Value (DV) tells you how much a nutrient in a serving contributes to a daily diet. Feasting on His Promises every day is recommended for heavenly nutritional health.

DESSERT

Promise Snacking

Take time to search the Word for more of the many promises of the Lord. Write them down on note cards or sticky notes, then hang them up all over your home where you can see them. Keep His promises front and center in your mind. Think of it like snacking throughout your day. This type of snacking will keep the weight of the world off you.

Reflection Questions

What is your favorite promise in the Word? Why is it your favorite?

What are some of the promises you see fulfilled in your life now?

Which promises are you still waiting for? What are you doing while you wait to see them fulfilled?

DAY 15

FEAST ON HIS VICTORY

Food for Thought: The Lord's army doesn't live off of military rations.

What then shall we say to these things? If God is for us, who can be against us?

Romans 8:31 (ESV)

Victory over Sin

I don't know about you, but I used to feel like I was constantly fighting my sinful self and the devil. Every time something bad happened, I immediately claimed it as an attack from the Enemy and got my fighting gear on. It was like I was getting ready for war. I remember the Lord spoke to me one day and gently pointed out how I give too much credit to the Enemy's power and the power of sin. Both sin and the devil are defeated. We do not need to battle for something the Lord has already won. The entire process of battle and victory is His.

I'm not saying that the Enemy won't try to attack. He does and he will continue to do so until he is locked away forever. What I'm saying is that we need to live in the understanding that the devil cannot win. It is impossible. This war and his fate were already determined when

Jesus died and rose again. Instead of striving in battle, we get to feast on Christ's spoils of war! We get to take our sword (His Word) and partner in His victory!

Attending Global Celebration School of Supernatural Ministry (GCSSM), I often heard this question, "Did someone forget to tell you that when Christ died, you died?" This question became a constant reminder of victory. I know that we feasted on being co-crucified during Day 9, but remember that His death on the cross finalized the victory over sin. Since you died with Him, He completely accomplished your victory over sin too. You no longer have to battle sin.

So, how do we live in victory over sin? Spend time feasting on Jesus! I want you to think about your identity when it comes to sin. Let's reflect on the following questions:

- What type of food is invading your thoughts?
  - » Is it junk food that focuses on not messing up and falling into sin?
  - » Is it true food that focuses on Jesus and how to draw closer to Him?

- How do you identify yourself?
  - » Are you identifying as a sinner or as a saint?

- What sort of relationship are you in?
  - » Are you in a "Sinship" (constantly thinking about and spending time with sin)?
  - » Are you in a "Sonship" (constantly thinking about and spending time with the Lord)?

Romans 6:6 says, "We know this: whatever we used to be with our old sinful ways has been nailed to His cross. So our entire record of sin has been canceled, and we no longer have to bow down to sin's power" (VOICE). Jesus gave us the victory through His death. Sin can no longer hold us captive. The only way sin has any power now is if we enter into relationship with it.

Why stay in a destructive relationship when you can be in holy union with *the* Holy One? This union takes you from an identity of a sinner to an identity of a saint (holy one)! You are a saint! You are a holy one! "Giving thanks to the Father who has qualified us to be *partakers of the inheritance of the saints* in the light" (Colossians 1:12, NKJV, italics added for emphasis).

Victory over the Enemy

 Hebrews 2:14-15 says, "Since we, the children, are all creatures of flesh and blood, Jesus took on flesh and blood, so that by dying He could destroy the one who held power over death—the devil—and destroy the fear of death that has always held people captive" (VOICE). No longer does the devil have any power over you. Through Jesus you were transferred from the domain of darkness and into His kingdom (Colossians 1:13). With this transfer came the power to resist the devil and see him crushed beneath your feet (Romans 16:20). The Enemy may come prowling and roaring like a lion, but he doesn't have any teeth anymore! The next time you feel attacked in your life, remember to keep your eyes on Jesus. When you feast on His victory, attacks begin to cease and desist because the Enemy has no authority over you anymore!

Victory Activation

The following activation you are about to read was inspired by Graham Cooke's book, *Manifesting Your Spirit*. I want you to take your time and visualize as you read. The Lord wants you activated to see His victory over every area of your life.

> *Imagine that you are like the servant of Elisha in 2 Kings 6. You step outside and there is a massive army surrounding you. There are so many warriors, and each one is enormous and seems immovable. Now, I want you to imagine that this army represents a problem. It can represent any problem in your life. The army in front of me represents cancer. The army carries banners that mock you with the*

name of your problem. The army is surrounding you, marching closer and closer, taunting you, and saying that it is impossible to defeat them. Their taunts start to get to you, and you feel and think about the impossibility of winning in this situation.

Suddenly, your eyes are drawn to look above the warriors' heads, and you see an army filled with chariots of fire. Leading this army is Jesus. He is smiling at you with the most peaceful smile. Jesus winks at you. Now you are filled with absolute faith and assurance that this enemy has already been completely defeated, they just don't know it yet. You start to shout the name of Jesus. "Jesus, Jesus, Jesus!" Joy wells up inside the core of who you are as you laugh and rejoice in victory in front of your enemy.

Suddenly, this army starts to shrink and look like ants before you. Fear covers the faces of the formerly gigantic warriors, and they tremble in terror. They back away from you. As you look down upon your defeated foes, Jesus' glory fills up the battlefield with such light that the enemy is completely blinded. Jesus comes to your side, gently places His hand on your hand, and together you touch the enemy. In an instant, the battlefield is wiped clean. Nothing remains of the army. You look around and where there was once trampled ground and decay, there is new growth and life. Jesus looks at you, smiles, and says, "Every battlefield you enter, every enemy you confront, I am with you, and I never lose."

It doesn't matter what seems impossible. No disease. No problem. Not even death has the victory over Jesus. As you stand in front of problems such as depression, lacking finances, or relationship issues, start to shout the name of Jesus and you will feel His power break out through you. He is your activator for victory. He mingles His hands and His words with yours. Touch that problem and watch it be completely obliterated from the battlefield.

When we recognize all that Jesus finished for us at the cross, we begin to understand why Paul wrote in 1 Corinthians 2:2, "For I determined to know nothing among you except Jesus Christ, and Him crucified" (NASB). If all I know is Jesus Christ and Him crucified, then all I know is His victory.

Victory Nutrition Label

Nutrition Facts

Unlimited servings per container

Serving size   **Overflowing cups**

Amount per serving

Christle

Consumption is a great source for

the following: **% Daily Value***

Living in victory over sin	100%
Living in victory over the Enemy	100%
Self-identifying as a saint	100%
Having joy in any circumstance	100%
Enjoying the spoils of war	100%
Claiming new spiritual territory	100%

*The % Daily Value (DV) tells you how much a nutrient in a serving contributes to a daily diet. Feasting on His Victory every day is recommended for heavenly nutritional health.

DESSERT

Victory March

God told Joshua and the Israelites to march around the city of Jericho for seven days before the city walls crumbled before them. They did a victory march even though they had not seen the victory yet. I want you to exercise during dessert today. Where do you need a victory in your life? March around your home however long you want, believing that this is your victory march. March around worshipping, praying, and feasting on His victory. God had the Israelites activate their faith by going on a victory march without evidence of the victory. Let's do the same.

Reflection Questions

How do you have victory over sin? How do you live in that victory?

What do you think when you read 1 Corinthians 2:2, "For I determined to know nothing among you except Jesus Christ, and Him crucified"? Write down your thoughts.

Glory Weight (n.)

What you gain after consuming more of the Lord, including His metabolism-boosting joy and protein-rich presence.

DAY 16

FEAST ON HIS GOODNESS

Food for Thought: How do you know when something tastes good? After eating it, you want everyone to taste it.

Taste and see that the Lord is good; How blessed is the man who takes refuge in Him!

Psalm 34:8 (NASB)

We are now halfway through our spiritual meal plans. How are you doing? I hope that you have experienced His glory like never before. This might be a good time to "weigh in" and see if you have lost some of the weight of depression, anxiety, and fear. Do you feel lighter? More energized? More joyful? I hope you have had this negative weight replaced with some "glory weight" as we have feasted on the Beloved and absorbed His nutrients. I am excited for you to discover more of what God has for you as we continue to dine on Him for the rest of our meal plans!

Define Goodness

Today we get to taste and see! This psalm for today specifically invites us to examine His goodness by tasting it. That means we need to experience the flavor of His goodness.

I told you a little of my testimony during Day 6's meal plan. I shared how I had become bitter and offended at God. What ultimately led to my bitterness and offense? I started to doubt the goodness of God. I had my definition of *good*, and I couldn't wrap my head around God not fitting into that definition. This allowed a voice of discord and doubt to come in and settle within my heart.

My breaking point toward offense at God came when my cousin Savannah died. She had become like a sister to me during my university days because my aunt, uncle, and cousins lived a lot closer to my school than my parents. I spent many of my school breaks with them. It was one of the best times in my life. Savannah was beautiful on the inside and outside, even though she dealt with hardship from the beginning of her life.

She was born without her spinal column forming properly. The medical term for this condition is Spina Bifida. Savannah spent a lot of time in and out of hospitals while she was growing up and experienced more hardship than most people do in a lifetime. She amazed me every time I was with her. Even though she couldn't do the things that others could do, she was never upset with God. She was always smiling. In fact, she spoke nothing but love to all who met her. The more time I spent with her, the more I thought to myself that this must be what spending time with Jesus is like. Love and peace flowed out of her and wrapped around anyone who was nearby.

All her life, my family believed in her complete healing on this earth. We didn't doubt at all. I never even considered that she would not walk and run here on this earth during my lifetime. So, when I received the phone call about her death, I didn't believe it. I couldn't believe it. I immediately booked a flight to America. The whole flight I was praying for a resurrection. It didn't happen. She stayed in heaven with her Beloved.

A tiny crack developed in my spiritual core. I started to doubt God's goodness. How could a good God let that happen? How could a good God allow the sweetest person I know to die while evil people live? How could a good God not do what His Word says and heal those that believe? This crack came and grew because God did not measure up to my definition of goodness. I defined goodness by my expectations and my understanding. Let me say this: God's goodness cannot be defined by human reasoning. God's goodness goes way beyond what we could possibly think or imagine. He sees everything in a way we could never see it.

> "My thoughts are nothing like your thoughts," says the Lord. "And my ways are far beyond anything you could imagine. For just as the heavens are higher than the earth, so my ways are higher than your ways and my thoughts higher than your thoughts."
>
> Isaiah 55:8-9 (NLT)

God's goodness is what brought me back to life after I had been living in my own hell of bitterness, offense, hatred, and despair. His goodness chased me down and never gave up on me. I realized that Savannah's death is not God's fault. We live in a broken corrupt world. This means that death, disasters, and decay exist in this world. Sin is what destroys lives. God did not cause sin. In His infinite goodness, He sent Christ to destroy sin.

I have said this before: I don't know why some live and others die, but I do know that God is good. We are not God, and we cannot know all that He knows. Sometimes, we allow the mysteries of why God does some things and not others to dissuade us from the true definition of goodness.

When I don't understand why things happen a certain way, I sit with Him at His table. I rest on His chest and ask Him for more of His wisdom—more of Him. I ask Him for glimpses of His understanding so that my lack of understanding will not become a stronghold of the Enemy. Romans 8:28 says, "We are confident that God is able to orchestrate everything to work toward something good and beautiful when we love Him and accept His invitation to live according to His plan" (VOICE).

When someone dies, do you believe His Word, or do you fall into despair in your lack of understanding? The answer: you stand by His Word and lean on *His* understanding! When disaster hits, do you blame God or recognize that the works of the devil are to seek, kill, and destroy? The answer: you recognize that God's heart is to restore, and that the devil is out for destruction.

In my heart I believe that God gave Savannah a choice. I believe that she could have come back to life here, but instead, she chose to stay with Jesus, the person she spent her whole life singing praises to. I know she is in heaven, running with the Lover of her soul. She is healed.

God's nature is goodness. He cannot do anything outside of His nature. Goodness is a fruit of His Spirit, which means we get to taste and see just how good it is.

Savor the Goodness

Let's take the last part of this meal and savor His goodness by focusing on who He is and what He does for us. Your breath is from the Lord. The sun that warms you, the crops that feed you, and the water that cleans you all come from Him. "Whatever is good and perfect is a gift coming down to us from God our Father, who created all the lights in the heavens. He never changes or casts a shifting shadow" (James 1:17, NLT). Each beat of your heart comes because He is good. Every tear you shed is caught and held because He is good. No matter what trials and troubles you face in this life, God is good. He gave His Son to set you free because He is good. He prepares a place for you at His table because He is good. He will never leave you because He is good. He gives you strength to overcome the world because He is good. "For the Lord God is a sun and shield; The Lord gives grace and glory; He withholds no good thing from those who walk with integrity" (Psalm 84:11, NASB). He loves you because He is good. He provides for you because He is good. He keeps the earth in motion because He is good.

When you do not understand why something bad happens, remember that evil does not come from Him. Instead, feast on His goodness. Praise Him for all that you have. Rejoice that He walks this life with you.

I want to end with a psalm from David. Even with all his hardships in life, he still wrote this beautiful verse for the Lord. Read it a few times and let it flow over you. God is a fountain of goodness. Rest in His arms, let that fountain wash over you, and drink it in.

> "I bless the holy name of God with all my heart. Yes, I will bless the Lord and not forget the glorious things he does for me. He forgives all my sins. He heals me. He ransoms me from hell. He surrounds me with loving-kindness and tender mercies. He fills my life with good things! My youth is renewed like the eagle's!"
>
> Psalm 103:1-5 (TLB)

Goodness Nutrition Label

Nutrition Facts

Unlimited servings per container

Serving size   **Overflowing cups**

Amount per serving

Christic

Consumption is a great source for the following: **% Daily Value***

Seeing His goodness flow out of you	100%
Knowing God does not produce evil	100%
Being secure with the mysteries of God	100%
Recognizing His goodness all the time	100%
Rejoicing in who He is	100%
Defining true goodness	100%

*The % Daily Value (DV) tells you how much a nutrient in a serving contributes to a daily diet. Feasting on His Goodness every day is recommended for heavenly nutritional health.

DESSERT

Goodness Sweets

I want you to create your own dessert today. We are going to chew on how good He is to us and create little goodness candies. Take time and write down all that God has done for you. Savor His goodness. His goodness knows no bounds; the more you chew on it, the more joy flows all around you.

Reflection Questions

How do you react when something negative happens in your life? What emotions arise from within you? Why do you react that way? Be honest with yourself and with God.

What comes to your mind when you think about the goodness of God? Why does that come to your mind?

SNACK TIME!

Deliverance

Let's take a moment to eat a little pre-meal snack. Deliverance is something that might seem complicated, but it is actually quite simple. Jesus shows us that deliverance is not a long, drawn-out process; it is deeply connected to intimacy with Him because He is freedom. When we know who is inside of us, we do not need to fear anything, struggle with addictions, or keep begging the Enemy to leave us alone.

Deliverance can happen in an instant. I have seen it happen with a hug. It doesn't matter if it is deliverance from sin, trauma, or demons. If you want to see people delivered, show them what relationship with Jesus looks like. We are supposed to use our authority and set the captives free. Our authority comes from Christ. We do not need to overcomplicate something that Jesus always restored and healed with simple commands. Deliverance is always found at the cross because that is where sin, death, and the Enemy were defeated. If we try to get people to look somewhere other than the cross, we end up putting more faith in the *process* of deliverance instead of the *Deliverer*.

> When He had *disarmed the rulers and authorities [those super-natural forces of evil operating against us]*, He made a public example of them [exhibiting them as captives in His triumphal procession], *having triumphed over them through the cross.*
>
> Colossians 2:15 (AMP, italics added for emphasis)

DAY 17

FEAST ON HIS FORGIVENESS

Food for Thought: If food smells rotten, looks rotten, and tastes rotten, it is rotten. This is also true of spiritual food.

God is faithful and reliable. If we confess our sins, he forgives them and cleanses us from everything we've done wrong.

1 John 1:9 (GW)

Forgive and Forget

I grew up hearing this simple statement: forgive and forget. This meant that once someone said they were sorry, it was no longer supposed to be held against them. We weren't supposed to remember the wrongdoing. Humans have a hard time trying to do this. I've tried to forgive and forget my whole life, but it never seemed to work in my own strength. I could not forget things without God stepping in and erasing them from my mind.

God is the expert at forgiving and choosing to forget. Hebrews 8:12 says, "For I will demonstrate my mercy to them and will forgive their evil deeds, and never remember again their sins" (TPT). His Word also says that He will not bring to His mind or mention your sins again (Jeremiah 31:34). If God does not want to remember our sins, why are we constantly reminding Him of them? Maybe it is because we do not recognize what His forgiveness truly is.

God's forgiveness is Him sending our sins away forever. "You see, God takes all our crimes—our seemingly inexhaustible sins—and removes them. As far as east is from the west, He removes them from us" (Psalm 103:12, VOICE). His forgiveness is Jesus coming and shedding His holy blood so that we might be free from the grasp of sin. His forgiveness is absolute once you repent. God is not like us. When we are hurt by someone, we can forgive them; but then if they do the same thing again, we recall the other times they have hurt us. God does not remember! He is not holding a grudge against you for your many transgressions. He is not sitting up in heaven waiting for you to mess up again. He is not on the edge of His throne ready to remind you of all the times you missed the mark.

I heard a comment about this during a class at Global Celebration. "If you missed the mark, you need to look at the mark on your hands where the nail that pierced Christ pierced you too." This mark of His crucifixion showcases His forgiveness and His finished work. God wants you to live a life free from regret, guilt, and shame. I do not recall those being among the list of the fruits of His Spirit. Feast on His forgiveness. Feast on His finished work and consume all that it means for you. Instead of guilt, we have joy. Instead of regret, we have delight. Instead of shame, we have honor. There is no junk food at His table! When Jesus took you to the grave with Him, He did not declare you half forgiven or half clean. He declared you a new creation (2 Corinthians 5.17).

This means that if the voices you hear don't sound like Jesus, look like Jesus, or feel like Jesus, they are not Jesus. Listening to those voices is like eating rotten food. It makes you sick and ineffective. Jesus wants a victorious bride, not a defeated one! The more you feast on Him and all that He has done for you, the more you recognize His voice. The more you recognize that His forgiveness is not incomplete or dependent on you

THE ULTIMATE FEAST · DAY 17

working for it. His forgiveness is a celebration! We simply recognize the wrong, repent, and then eat at His table!

Forgive All

There are many places in the Bible that mention forgiving others because God forgave us (Colossians 3:13 and Ephesians 4:31-32 to name just a few). In Matthew 18:21-22, Peter asked Jesus if he should forgive someone up to seven times, and Jesus declares not seven, but seventy times seven! Jesus said this to show that it is not about numbers; it is about showcasing God's heart of forgiveness, which is limitless.

When people hurt us, we forgive them. However, that does not mean that we do not set up boundaries. God doesn't want us to be punching bags for anyone. He wants us to live life abundantly. Sometimes, that means we need to separate from certain people. We still pray for them. We still love them. We still forgive them. But we do not give them direct access to continually wound us.

The more we feast on His forgiveness, the more we will experience His character of forgiveness flowing out of us. What does this mean? It means that when people hurt us, we not only forgive them, but God will restore our thoughts toward them to be better than ever! Instead of thinking about certain individuals and feeling pain and anger, you can think about them and feel love and excitement to be with them. I cannot forget the wrongs others have done to me on my own, but God can take all that wrong and make it better. If you want to know how to truly forgive others, feast on His forgiveness. It is supernatural; there is no wound it cannot heal or broken relationship it cannot fix.

There is one more part to this meal plan. You need to be able to forgive all, which includes yourself. Can you look at your past and feel peace about it? Do you now have joy when you think of where you have been? I'm talking about all of your past—even the places where you made mistakes. I think of it like this: the Paula who made all the mistakes, who turned people away from the Lord, who harbored bitterness and offense at God—that Paula doesn't exist anymore. When I asked God for His for-giveness, she ceased to be. "The old way of living has disappeared. A new way of living has come into existence" (2 Corinthians 5:17b, GW). A new Paula was put into existence. As the new Paula, I get to live an entirely different life because I have the Spirit of Jesus in me. This means that I am no longer tied to my past identity. I am no longer the woman defined by her mess. I am now the woman who is defined by Christ's holiness.

Does this mean that I go back to live a life in sin and say it's covered by Christ's forgiveness? No! Repentance comes before forgiveness. In Acts 3:19 we are told to repent, and then turn to God. Part of repentance is turning from sin and going in a different direction. My new existence can find no pleasure in sin. The Spirit of Jesus in me will *not* coexist with sin.

Forgiveness is realizing that we made a mistake, admitting it, and then walking as if we are new. If God does not remember our mistakes, then we should likewise forgive ourselves and stop living in the past. It is so much better to live at His table and consume all that He has for us, now and forever.

Forgiveness Nutrition Label

Nutrition Facts

Unlimited servings per container

Serving size   **Overflowing cups**

Amount per serving

Christabel

Consumption is a great source for the following: **% Daily Value***

Living free from past mistakes	100%
Knowing how to forgive all	100%
Creating better relationships	100%
Showing others they are forgiven	100%
Existing as a new creation	100%
Recognizing rotten food	100%

*The % Daily Value (DV) tells you how much a nutrient in a serving contributes to a daily diet. Feasting on His Forgiveness every day is recommended for heavenly nutritional health.

DESSERT

From Mess to Message

I want us to take time to celebrate how God has forgiven us! There is so much mess that the Lord has brought you out of, and now it turns into your message of His goodness. Write down five things that are no longer a part of your identity. Then I want you to tear them up and throw them in the air like confetti! God has already torn these up. This is to symbolize and come into agreement with what He has already accomplished in you. Celebrate His forgiveness and rejoice in the new you!

Reflection Questions

Do you have someone in your life you still might need to forgive? This can also include yourself. You can tell based on how you think about them/yourself and how you talk about them/yourself. Are your thoughts and words about them/yourself negative or positive? Be honest. God wants us to live in His forgiveness which includes forgiving *all*.

One of the best ways to learn how to forgive is to feast on His love. I recommend that you go back and read Day 1. Love does not keep a record of offenses (1 Corinthians 13:5).

How do you feel when you read that God removes your sins as far as the east is from the west? What does this mean to you as you live out every day?

DAY 18

FEAST ON HIS GLORY

Food for Thought: If our body requires food every day, then should we not feed our spirit every day?

For everything comes from him and exists by his power and is intended for his glory. All glory to him forever! Amen.

Romans 11:36 (NLT)

Glory through Wonders

I'm going to be honest; God's glory is hard to explain with words. This is why I'm so grateful that He chooses to showcase His glory with His creation. How do we feast on His glory? Look around and see the radiance of who He is in the splendor of His creation. Think about His glory while you walk around outside. The sun is so bright that we cannot look directly at it, yet His glory has more radiance. The ocean is so vast that we have not explored it all, yet His glory has no measure. Flowers are draped with the most elaborate colors, yet the extravagance of His glory cannot be dcfincd. Mountains stand as displays of grandeur, yet they are tiny specks compared to His majesty. The universe is filled with undiscovered phenomena, yet it pales in comparison to the wonders of

His glory! God wants us to see how glorious He is, which is why He made such a beautiful display of His glory. "The heavens proclaim the glory of God. The skies display his craftsmanship" (Psalm 19:1 NLT).

We see glimpses of God's glory in the Old Testament when He appeared as a pillar of cloud by day and a pillar of fire by night (Exodus 13). Then after Moses went to speak with God on Mount Sinai, his face shone because God's glory left a residue on him (Exodus 34). A little later, God covered the tabernacle with a cloud and filled it with His glory (Exodus 40:34).

To me, it was like God was trying to get closer and closer to His people. The closer people got to God's glory, the more it produced a change in them. David feasted on God's glory everywhere he went. How do we know? Because David gave praises to the Lord. He described God's glory in creation and through his own experiences. When people encounter the glory of God, they cannot help but stand in awe of Him. They praise Him for all that His is and all that He does. They worship Him. God's glory is like a shroud that represents His triumph, His mighty wonders, and His splendor. When you encounter that glory, you cannot help but be changed.

When I worship God with my whole being, I encounter that glory. It surrounds me; it envelopes me; it swallows me up. Nothing else exists in that moment but God and me. I don't care what I look or sound like; all I care about is Him and feasting on His glory as I praise Him. For a long time, I did care about what I looked like during worship. I ended up missing out on experiencing the fullness of His glory because I was too focused on others. I encourage you, if you want to experience God's glory, get rid of what I will call the "people-pleasing spirit." It doesn't matter what people think about you during worship. Worship isn't about them. Worship isn't even about you. It is about God, His presence, His glory, and His magnificence. If you can fully focus on Him, you will see His glory on display.

Glory through Christ

God revealed His glory through Jesus Christ in the New Testament. "He is the *radiance of the glory of God* and the *exact imprint of his nature*, and he upholds the universe by the word of his power. After making purification for sins, he sat down at the right hand of the Majesty on high" (Hebrews 1:3, ESV, italics added for emphasis). I love this verse. Christ is the radiance of the glory of God! Jesus displayed God's glory everywhere He went. He healed the sick, which showed He held the power over all disease. He raised the dead, which showed His triumph over death. He called the storms to cease, which showed His authority over the earth. He now sits at the right hand of God, which shows He is above all authorities and powers in existence. Through Jesus, God gets ultimate glory. Jesus freely gave up His divine regality to become human. He then died a criminal's death.

> "Yet it was because of this that God raised him up to the heights of heaven and gave him a name which is above every other name, that at the name of Jesus every knee shall bow in heaven and on earth and under the earth, and every tongue shall confess that Jesus Christ is Lord, to the glory of God the Father"
>
> Philippians 2:9-11 (TLB).

Everything about Jesus points us to the glory of God. Because of Jesus, we get to intimately experience and feast on God's glory. Jesus is how we know the fullness of God. Jesus is how we have intimacy with God. For so long, the Israelites had to keep a safe distance from God, but we get to dwell in the cloud of His glory through Jesus!

I'm going to wrap up this meal with another treat. I wanted to give glory to my Lord, my Friend, and my Beloved. I noticed that as I gave Him glory, honor, and praise, I feasted on His glory. I got to experience His deep love, majesty, and splendor as I wrote this, so I wanted to share it with you. While you read it, I pray images, feelings, and deeper revelations come to you.

To the One

To the One who spoke and life burst into existence.

To the One who parted the seas to freedom.

To the One who can stop the sun and moon for a victory.

To the One who left His throne for the sake of humanity.

To the One who became sin to destroy sin.

To the One who died to overthrow death.

To the One who tore the veil and granted access to heaven.

To the One who rose to life to give others resurrection life.

To the One who proposed union from the beginning of time.

To the One who loves unconditionally.

To the One who invites me to His banqueting table.

To the One in whom my life truly begins.

To You be all the glory.

Glory Nutrition Label

Nutrition Facts

Unlimited servings per container

Serving size   **Overflowing cups**

Amount per serving

Christic

Consumption is a great source for the following: **% Daily Value***

Getting lost in the wonders of God	100%
Being changed from the inside out	100%
Destroying the "people-pleasing spirit"	100%
Dwelling in the cloud of His glory	100%
Having a heart filled with praise	100%
Praising, even if it be undignified	100%

*The % Daily Value (DV) tells you how much a nutrient in a serving contributes to a daily diet. Feasting on His Glory every day is recommended for heavenly nutritional health.

DESSERT

Glory Toast

I want you to raise your glass to the Lord. You can look at my example, *To the One*, but I want you to write your own toast and give glory to God. He deserves it. No matter what is happening in your life, God is good and deserves to be praised. When we glorify Him in all circumstances, things start to shift in our lives. Something shifts in your spirit. Write out your toast and then say it aloud to Him.

Reflection Questions

How do you see God's glory in nature? Write down a few examples. How do those examples showcase God's glory?

In your own words, write down how Jesus displays God's glory. Use Scripture references. Why does this display God's glory?

DAY 19

FEAST ON HIS HOLINESS

Food for Thought: If food purifiers remove bacteria and other harmful substances, then Jesus is the ultimate food purifier!

Each of these living beings had six wings, and their wings were covered all over with eyes, inside and out. Day after day and night after night they keep on saying, *"Holy, holy, holy is the Lord God, the Almighty— the one who always was, who is, and who is still to come."*

Revelation 4:8 (NLT, italics added for emphasis)

He IS the I AM

In today's meal plan we are going to marinate in the holiness of God and what that means for us. Remember, God invites all believers to come dine with Him. "They will come from east and west, from north and south, to share the banquet in the kingdom of God" (Luke 13:29, CSB). When we sit at His table, we are sitting in holiness—His purity, His perfection, and His sanctification.

Take a moment right now and say those words that the living beings say in Revelation 4:8: *Holy, holy, holy is the Lord God, the Almighty–the one who always was, who is, and who is to come.* Say it again. Say it a third time. There is a reason that the book of Revelation tells us these words are being declared day and night without ceasing. Something happens when you declare God's holiness. You take it into yourself and become invigorated. God cannot be tainted. He cannot be corrupted. He cannot be led astray. He IS the I AM. That means He is everything that is good, just, holy, faithful, pure, kind, gentle, loving, and more.

Some people think that because God is holy, He is unreachable. The truth is, in His holiness, God is the One reaching out to us with arms wide open. He never wanted to be separate from us. He was devastated when sin corrupted us. But His holiness will not allow sin to exist within His presence; God's holiness destroys sin automatically. This is why Uzzah died immediately when he tried to steady the Ark of the Covenant (2 Samuel 6:7). God's holiness cannot be touched by a corrupted nature, even with the best of intentions. His holiness will not allow it.

When I read the Old Testament, I'm so grateful for Jesus because He is our gateway to direct relationship with God. Before Christ, our corrupted nature could not come near God's holiness. It was impossible. This is why God designed the veil to keep the Holy of Holies separated. Exodus 33 tells us that Moses placed the Tent of Meeting outside of Israel's encampment in the wilderness. Moses understood the power and virtue of God's holiness and that the "stiff-necked" (Exodus 33:3) people could not live near it.

Yet, as we have already discussed, God longed for intimacy with us. Jesus in His holy nature gives us a new incorruptible nature that is already sanctified by His blood. Jesus took your unholy nature, crucified it on the cross, buried it, and then raised you up a new creature. His eternal, holy nature inhabits the new you. I love to sit at His table, close my eyes, and declare:

Holy, Holy, Holy is the Lord. You are my beginning and my end. You are the first and the last. You are my everything.

Deconstructed Sanctification

Have you ever eaten deconstructed food? Deconstructed food is where chefs change the appearance of the food but keep the overall flavors the same. I used to think this was odd, but then I realized you can sometimes taste the flavor more intensely in deconstructed food because you are not caught up in what the food should look like. The flavors are the focus.

A few years ago, the Lord started to deconstruct sanctification for me. I know this can sound bad because many people want to deconstruct the Word and Christianity, but I'm not talking about tearing apart sanctification. I'm talking about savoring the flavors of His holiness through sanctification. I grew up believing that holiness is a process that is never achieved until we die. I was supposed to strive to be holy, and I would always be fighting to be sanctified little by little.

This is not what the Word says though. "And by that will, we have been *made holy* through the sacrifice of the body of Jesus Christ once for all" (Hebrews 10:10, NIV, italics added for emphasis). It is by the blood of Jesus that we receive sanctification, not through our own efforts. "And some of you used to be like this. But you *were washed*, you *were sanctified*, you *were justified* in the name of the Lord Jesus Christ and by the Spirit of our God" (1 Corinthians 6:11, CSB). I emphasized these parts in this scripture because they are past tense.

If we are not considered holy once we accept Jesus as Lord and Savior, then how can God's Spirit dwell in us? God is everything that is holy, and because He is holy, nothing tainted with sin can come near Him. The holiness of God destroys anything that is not pure. Knowing this, God calls us to be holy like Him. "But be holy *now* in everything you do, just as the Lord is holy, who invited you to be his child. He himself has said, 'You must be holy, for I am holy'" (1 Peter 1:15-16, TLB, italics added for emphasis).

How do we accept this call to holiness? Through Jesus. Jesus is how we get to be holy. Jesus took all our impurities upon Himself and then demolished them. We are now washed spotless by the perfect blood of Jesus. When we were covered in sin, we could not cross the veil into the Holy of Holies because nothing tainted by sin or evil could enter. Jesus took you and purified you through the baptism of His death. He destroyed everything that corrupted you.

What does this mean for us now? We get to feast on His holiness! We get to live in His intimacy and His presence. We get to share in His holiness because Jesus made us holy! We are no longer considered sinners but are called saints. Paul addresses many of his letters to "the saints." The meaning of the word "saint" is *holy one*. I have read the Bible repeatedly, but it was only after I started feasting on the Lord and all He has done that I realized He calls us His saints. The Lord does not address us as "those who will one day be saints."

I don't know about you, but I felt like a huge burden was taken from me when I understood that Jesus already sanctified me, and I'm not in the process of trying to do it myself. I get to rest in His holiness and let it wash over me. This is also how I lead a holy life. I don't have to "watch out for sin" anymore. I just keep my eyes on my Beloved, and sin is nowhere to be found. Sit and feast on His holiness and watch as it becomes a part of you.

Holiness Nutrition Label

Nutrition Facts

Unlimited servings per container

Serving size   **Overflowing cups**

Amount per serving

Christ

Consumption is a great source for the following: **% Daily Value***

Basking in the awe of God	100%
Living in intimacy with the I AM	100%
Crushing the idea of self-sanctification	100%
Being wrapped in God's holiness	100%
Realizing you are already holy	100%
Living a holy life now	100%

*The % Daily Value (DV) tells you how much a nutrient in a serving contributes to a daily diet. Feasting on His Holiness every day is recommended for heavenly nutritional health.

DESSERT

Pickling Process

There was a Greek poet and physician named Nicander who lived around 200 B.C.[7] Nicander wrote a text, which included a recipe for making pickles. In this recipe he used the word *baptizô* (baptized) to describe immersing the vegetable in the vinegar solution. The word *baptizo* is specifically used because it indicates a permanent change. Once the vegetable is baptized in the solution, it comes out an entirely new creation; it comes out a pickle.

This same word is used in Romans 6:3 which says, "Do you not know that all of us who have been *baptized* into Christ Jesus were *baptized* into his death?" (ESV, italics added for emphasis). You have been pickled! You were permanently changed when you were baptized into Jesus. Pickles can never return to being cucumbers once they have been baptized!

After reading about this pickling process and Romans 6:3, how do you see yourself as permanently changed?

---

7   Sourced from blueletterbible.org—additional information G907

Reflection Questions

Read 1 Corinthians 1:30: "God has united you with Christ Jesus. For our benefit God made him to be wisdom itself. Christ made us right with God; he made us pure and holy, and he freed us from sin" (NLT). What does this scripture mean to you?

How are you pure and holy?

How are you freed from sin?

How do you live as a saint now?

Journey to the wine cellar and take a drink of His New Wine!

Suddenly, he transported me into his
house of wine—he looked upon me with
his unrelenting love divine.

Song of Songs 2:4 (TPT)

DAY 20

FEAST ON HIS FREEDOM

Food for Thought: [8]If waiting for death is how we will be free from sin once and for all, then we have now crowned death as our savior instead of Jesus Christ.

So if the Son makes you free, then you are unquestionably free.

John 8:36 (AMP)

Free to Live Free

For today's meal there should be trumpets sounding while we feast. Trumpets should announce the freedom that Christ has brought to His people and the celebration that goes with it. I am not the same person I was before Christ. I am His new creation and the battle with sin and death is finished!

During Day 2 we feasted on His finished work. That is the beginning of our freedom. The cross and the resurrection liberated us from the cycles and bondages of sin. Are you living in freedom today? I said this on Day 2, and I'll say it again here: only people who are free can set others

---

8   Food for Thought inspired by Clarke's Commentary on Romans chapter 8.

free. We live in freedom because we recognize the truth of Jesus' finished work. "And you shall know the truth, and the truth shall *make you free*" (John 8:32, NKJV, italics added for emphasis).

We have been chewing on all Jesus has done for us and to us for 19 days so far. The truth of what Jesus has already accomplished is our freedom. Your cycle of sin was broken at the cross. Are you living in that truth today, or are you listening to a small voice that says you are always going to battle sin? If we are constantly battling sin, we are not free. We are either slaves to sin or slaves to righteousness (Romans 6:16-18). Not both.

I learned a few years ago to recognize the voice that was trying to take my freedom. I can recognize it because it sounds condemning. It never brings hope. It never brings solutions. It makes me feel heavier. It makes me feel trapped. That is not Jesus. Jesus is hope. Jesus takes your burdens; He doesn't increase them. The truth is found in Romans 8:1-2, "So there is now no condemnation awaiting those who belong to Christ Jesus. For the power of the life-giving Spirit—and this power is mine through Christ Jesus—has freed me from the vicious circle of sin and death" (TLB). Christ did it for you! He freed us from the sin cycles that have plagued us for so long.

If you hear a voice (whether in your mind or through others) that is condemning you, it is not Jesus. Jesus convicts us; He does not condemn us. Conviction always comes with a solution, and it gives you hope that you can be free from your mistakes. 1 John 3:9 says, "No one born of God makes a practice of sinning, for God's seed abides in him; and he cannot keep on sinning, because he has been born of God" (ESV). We don't have to keep sinning! Jesus doesn't remember your sins after you admit your wrongs. This is freeing! It means that we are not living life with labels like "liar," "addict," "adulterer," or "bad parent." Christ doesn't remember your mistakes or keep them logged against you! He labels you like this: "my bride," "worthy," "loved," "holy," and "beautiful." So, when that little voice starts to infiltrate your freedom, recognize it, call it out, and shut it up. It is not even worth listening to.

Let me share an example with you about my daughter concerning her identity. One day, my daughter came to me and told me a lie. I knew she lied because I saw her commit the misdeed she claimed she did not do. I could have called her a liar and labeled her as one, but that is not who she is. She is *not* a liar. She has the truth of Jesus inside her, and He wants the truth to flow out of her. Christ sees her as a truth teller. What would happen to my daughter's identity if I called her a liar? I believe that she would start to see herself as a liar and then live up to expectations as a liar.

But, since I call her a truth teller, she starts to tell me the truth because she sees herself as truthful and lives up to the expectations of a truth teller. She begins to understand her true identity. It is important to recognize the truth and draw it out by speaking it. The truth is what sets us free. The truth is that our mistakes are not our identity. Jesus is our identity. I'm not graded on my performance anymore. I'm graded on *His* performance. When we make mistakes, we acknowledge them, make them right, and move on. We don't dwell on them or live like God is still holding them against us. He's not. He freed you from them through Jesus! Just like our verse for today's meal says, "If the Son makes you free, you are unquestionably free!"

Free to Free Others

I love this verse in 2 Corinthians 3:17, "For the Lord is the Spirit, and wherever the Spirit of the Lord is, there is freedom" (NLT). Guess what? The Spirit of the Lord now dwells in you because we receive the Holy Spirit when we accept Jesus! This means that you carry freedom inside of you, and you get to share it everywhere you go. I often have people come up to me and ask me why I am so happy, bold, and different. I tell them it's because I believe Galatians 2:20 (I have been crucified with Christ), Colossians 2:10 (I have been made complete in Christ), and 2 Corinthians 5:17 (I have become a new creation). I believed the truth of these verses and it set me free. Once I realized that the Word is my truth, it became my reality, which changed me from the inside out. People see the freedom I have in Christ, and it is attractive to them. When we live a life that demonstrates the gospel—the *good news* gospel—people want to know more about it. They want to taste it. I walk in freedom because I walk with Jesus. He isn't just a 20-minute, daily routine. He is a 24/7 partner for life. The more time you spend with Jesus, the more freedom you experience. You see all that He finished at the cross, and then you have the privilege of showing others who Christ is in you.

I just want to mention one more note here on our freedom meal plan. The religious leaders during the days of the apostles used the law to enslave the people. They promoted doctrines that included man-made requirements and work-based efforts to receive salvation. These doctrines still exist today and will destroy freedom. I grew up believing that if I didn't get an A+ on my spiritual report card, I would never see God move in my life. Or that by living a life separated from worldly things, I was better or holier than others. These doctrines keep you focused on yourself and your works instead of on Jesus and His finished work.

Paul gives us great advice in Galatians 5:1, "So Christ has truly set us free. Now make sure that you stay free, and don't get tied up again in slavery to the law" (NLT). Keeping our eyes on Jesus is how we live a life filled with freedom and celebration. I feel like I am constantly enjoying a victory party. I love to invite others to come, sit at His table, and enjoy the party with me. When we are free, we get to help others become free. Let the trumpets sound!

Freedom Nutrition Label

Nutrition Facts

Unlimited servings per container

Serving size   **Overflowing cups**

Amount per serving

Christation

Consumption is a great source for the following: **% Daily Value***

Losing the weight of the world	100%
Recognizing voices that are not Jesus	100%
Aligning with Jesus' identity	100%
Helping others step into freedom	100%
Never going back into bondage	100%
Hearing trumpets sound all the time	100%

*The % Daily Value (DV) tells you how much a nutrient in a serving contributes to a daily diet. Feasting on His Freedom every day is recommended for heavenly nutritional health.

DESSERT

Free Range Protein

It is time to take the truth outside the four walls of the church or even your own house. The world needs free-range protein. The world needs a good news gospel to be demonstrated. I want you to find someone today or this week that you can speak freedom into. Ask the Holy Spirit for a prophetic word of freedom for someone you meet at the grocery store, work, on the street, pumping gas, etc. Share your freedom in Christ with them by showing them what freedom looks like. Find someone then take a minute and ask the Lord for a word for them. Go speak the word without adding your own interpretation. The word should be encouraging, comforting, and positive.

Reflection Questions

Describe how you are free in Christ. Write down at least three powerful statements. For example: I am no longer a slave to sin.

Take a moment and sit with the Lord and ask Him for five words that describe you. These words will be positive. Write them down and savor them. This is how He sees you.

What can you do to make sure you don't get "tied up again in slavery to the law" (Galatians 5:1)?

DAY 21

FEAST ON HIS PERSPECTIVE

> **Food for Thought:** Perhaps if we feast on the treasures of heaven, we might see more of heaven.

Yes, feast on all the treasures of the heavenly realm and fill your thoughts with heavenly realities, and not with the distractions of the natural realm.

Colossians 3:2 (TPT)

Jesus' Perspective

Have you ever sat and wondered how Jesus sees things? How does He view your life? How does He see your family? Coworkers? Ministry? What does His perspective look like? How does it compare with that of the world?

Let's look at some examples in the Word. When the world saw an adulteress, Jesus saw a woman who could be faithful (John 8). When the world saw a cheat and a liar, Jesus saw a generous and truthful man (Zaccheus; Luke 19). When the world saw a leprous man, Jesus saw a clean and healthy man (Matthew 8). When the world saw a storm, Jesus saw peace (Mark 4:39). When the world saw utter defeat, Jesus saw total victory (crucifixion and resurrection).

Let's look at Jesus' perspective today. When the world sees death and decay, Jesus sees life and restoration. When the world sees victims, Jesus sees victors. The world may see all your mistakes, but Jesus sees your perfection. The world may see your dirtiness, but Jesus sees your purity. The world may see your sickness, but Jesus sees your wholeness. The world may see your failures, but Jesus sees your successes. The world may see you as lacking, but Jesus sees you as more than enough.

Take a moment and feast on His perspective. It is completely contrary to the world's. He doesn't look at the problems in our lives, He looks at the solutions. I'm so glad that Jesus has heaven's perspective because He invites us to share His perspective with Him.

Where does Jesus keep His eyes focused? On the Father. Jesus tells us that He does what He sees the Father doing (John 5:19). Because Jesus kept focusing on the Father, He knew that everything He needed would be provided. He also knew that sickness would disappear before Him. He knew that there was joy set before Him at the cross. Jesus knew that victory was already set in place because He kept His eyes on the Father.

In Matthew 6:22 Jesus says, "The eye is the lamp of the body. So, if your eye is healthy, your whole body will be full of light" (ESV). If we keep our eyes focused on the Lord, then we will do what He does, and see as He sees. Our perspective affects everything about us: how we think, feel, and act. Let's keep our eyes healthy by seeing in the manner that Jesus sees.

Seated in Heavenly Places

When we are born again, we are also seated with Christ in heavenly places (Ephesians 2:6). This means that our perspective changes to match Christ's perspective. I think about it like this: when I am standing in a field, I can only see what is directly around me; when I am seated in heaven looking down on the field, I have a wider, fuller perspective.

Often, we get focused on what is directly happening in front of us, and we cannot see the whole picture. When my husband was sick and hospitalized for months in Japan, all I saw was him getting sicker and sicker. I couldn't see God taking what the Enemy meant for evil and using it for good. Let me say this. God did not make James sick or keep him sick. God's will is to heal and heal He did.

While James was hospitalized, I saw people open their hearts to the Lord who had previously refused to acknowledge there was a God. If I would have had a heavenly perspective, I could have seen that this sickness was only temporary—Jesus already defeated Crohn's. I would have seen that health and wholeness were in our future.

When we know that we are seated in heavenly places, our perspective is from heaven. We clearly see the solution to every problem because right next to us is Jesus. He is the solution to every problem. If things don't look good, you are looking in the wrong place. It is as simple as that. 2 Corinthians 4:18 says, "So we don't look at the troubles we can see now; rather, we fix our gaze on things that cannot be seen. For the things we see now will soon be gone, but the things we cannot see will last forever" (NLT). The things that happen to us now are only temporary. Remember, victory belongs to the Lord. He has already made you more than a conqueror (Romans 8:37). Overcoming is not something you *do*, but who you *are* because of Christ in you. In 2023, I attended a healing room conference where Cal Pierce once said it like this: "When you live in the Answer, you won't see the problem." Jesus is the answer to everything you need. He is where our eyes should focus. All we must do is turn and look right next to us, because He is seated right there. "Let us keep our eyes fixed on Jesus, on whom our faith depends from beginning to end" (Hebrews 12:2a, GNT).

When I was little, my church would sometimes sing old hymns. I used to think they were boring until I started to chew on the words. There is so much revelation and power in many old hymns. I want to share the lyrics of an old hymn written by Helen Howarth Lemmel. I want you to read these lyrics and just savor the words.

Turn Your Eyes Upon Jesus

O soul are you weary and troubled
No light in the darkness you see
There's light for a look at the Savior
And life more abundant and free

Turn your eyes upon Jesus
Look full in his wonderful face
And the things of earth will grow strangely dim
In the light of his glory and grace

His word shall not fail you he promised
Believe him and all will be well
Then go to a world that is dying
His perfect salvation to tell

Turn your eyes upon Jesus
Look full in his wonderful face
And the things of earth will grow strangely dim
In the light of his glory and grace

Keep your eyes upon Jesus and the things of this earth will lose their focus because your eyes will be filled with His wonder and majesty. Keep your eyes on Jesus and your life will be free!

Perspective Nutrition Label

Nutrition Facts

Unlimited servings per container

Serving size   **Overflowing cups**

Amount per serving

Christ

Consumption is a great source for the following: **% Daily Value***

Seeing the victory instead of the battle	100%
Knowing what heaven looks like	100%
Staying healthy and happy	100%
Identifying junk food from true food	100%
Fixing your eyes on the cross	100%
Seeing simplicity instead of difficulty	100%

*The % Daily Value (DV) tells you how much a nutrient in a serving contributes to a daily diet. Feasting on His Perspective every day is recommended for heavenly nutritional health.

DESSERT

Prophetic Art

Prophetic art is a great way to see things from different perspectives. I want you to get something that you can create with. It can be colored pencils, paint, an art program on a tablet, etc. Put on some worship music and create some prophetic art based on what you hear, see, or feel. Once you are finished, ask the Lord what it means.

Changing Perspectives

I love pictures, and perspective is a vital part of getting a great photo. I want you to try changing perspectives while taking pictures. This activates us to see how God's perspective is much greater than ours. Take your cell phone or a camera and try taking pictures from these three different perspectives.

1. Instead of taking a picture straight ahead or at eye level, take a photo of an object pointing the lens up or down. You will capture new perspectives.
2. Take a photo of an object while looking through something like a fence, window, or a glass. This will give you a completely unique perspective.
3. Use a reflective surface to change your perspective. You can take a photo using a mirror, water, window, or anything that reflects.

After you try this, I want you to remember that how we see things can greatly shift just by changing our perspective.

DAY 22

FEAST ON HIS BLISS

> **Food for Thought:** We don't need man-made preservatives to keep us safe from spiritual decay. Jesus does that.

Oh the *bliss* of him whose guilt is pardoned, and his sin forgiven! Oh the *bliss* of him whom the Eternal has absolved, whose spirit has made full confession!

Psalm 32:1-2 (Moffat, italics added for emphasis)

Ecstasy of Salvation

Let's start today's feast by munching on some meanings of the word *bliss*:

Bliss (Merriam-Webster.com)
Complete happiness • Paradise, Heaven
Bliss (Dictionary.com)
Supreme happiness; utter joy or contentment • The joy of heaven
Bliss (Thefreedictionary.com)
Extreme happiness; ecstasy • The ecstasy of salvation; spiritual joy

I first heard bliss defined as the ecstasy of salvation while listening to Winnie Banov during a class at GCSSM. I had never heard bliss used that way, and I never imagined a feeling of ecstasy when I thought of salvation. I viewed salvation as a way to get out of hell. I never imagined it as an ongoing party to celebrate my new life in Christ.

Listening to Winnie, I started to understand that salvation wasn't just a "get out of hell" ticket. It is an invitation to unite with Christ in a life filled with complete happiness and the joy of heaven! "For the Lord God is a Sun and Shield; the Lord bestows [present] grace and favor and [future] glory (honor, splendor, and *heavenly bliss*)! No good thing will He withhold from those who walk uprightly" (Psalm 84:11, AMPC, italics added for emphasis). God gives us heavenly bliss! You have nothing good withheld from you! Christ didn't die just to save us from destruction. That was only part of it. He died so that we might walk in the fullness of life (Ephesians 3:19).

Christ doesn't just restore us to a right standing with God, He also transplants us next to His river of blessing when we feast on Him and mediate on His Word. Psalm 1:3 says this about us, "He will be standing firm like a flourishing tree planted by God's design, deeply rooted by the brooks of *bliss*, bearing fruit in every season of life. He is never dry, never fainting, ever blessed, ever prosperous" (TPT, italics added for emphasis). Part of our ecstasy of salvation is that we are fruitful all the time, no matter what is happening around us. We don't have to fear drought, recession, or sickness because He *saved* us from the ways of this world and has given us entry into the supernatural ways of His realm.

Believers in Jesus are no longer restricted by the fallen natural order of things. We now access the perfected supernatural order of heavenly things. Let's marinate and soak in this bliss. Let Jesus' bliss, His extreme happiness, be absorbed into your entire being. I don't want you to look at this like an Instapot moment. Don't just sit with Jesus for ten minutes and say your meal is ready. Steep yourself in Him for hours, days, weeks, years, eternity. The longer you steep, the more you will soak in the bliss of Jesus. If you haven't been filled to the brim with the ecstasy of His embrace, then I encourage you to go into His wine cellar and drink! "He has brought me to the house of wine; his banner raised over me is love" (Song of Songs 2:4, CEB). Drink Him in! Let Him overwhelm you with His thoughts toward you.

Feel the Bliss

Now it is time to revel in the bliss of Jesus! I pray that as you read the following statements, you will have the joy of heaven descend upon you!

- You were the joy set before Him at the cross.
- When Christ died, you died.
- He erased all your sins, guilt, and shame at the cross.
- When Christ was buried, you were buried.
- When you were baptized into Jesus' death, you became a part of Him.
- When Christ was resurrected, you were resurrected.
- The old you doesn't exist anymore.
- You have been raised to a new life and have entered into union with Jesus.
- You are fearfully and wonderfully made.
- You are unique to the kingdom.
- You have been planted in His holiness.
- There is nothing standing between you and God.
- You have become the dwelling place of the Eternal One.
- You have full access to the realities of heaven.
- You are not a mistake.
- You have the right to be joyful!
- You are a holy one!
- You are saved!
- You are free!
- You are complete!

Now make your own bliss statements by filling in the blanks with the truth as found in Christ. May the joy of heaven flood your room as you experience more bliss.

Personal Bliss Statements

I am _____!

Jesus destroyed _____ on the cross!

I am no longer a _____ but now a _____!

_____ is my portion!

Christ has set me free from _____ and I am free indeed!!

"For the Lord alone is my Savior. What a feast of favor and *bliss* he gives his people."

Psalm 3:8 (TPT, italics added for emphasis)

Bliss Nutrition Label

Nutrition Facts

Unlimited servings per container

Serving size   **Overflowing cups**

Amount per serving

Christ

Consumption is a great source for

the following: **% Daily Value***

Living in the ecstasy of salvation	100%
Experiencing the joy of heaven	100%
Cleansing the palate of misery	100%
No more Instapot moments with Jesus	100%
Bearing fruit in every season	100%
Uncontrollable bouts of laughter	100%

*The % Daily Value (DV) tells you how much a nutrient in a serving contributes to a daily diet. Feasting on His Bliss every day is recommended for heavenly nutritional health.

DESSERT

Bliss-filled Treats

For today's dessert we are going to create some bliss-filled treats and pass them on to people. I want you to think of three people you know that could use some extreme happiness in their life. Now, I want you to write 2-3 powerful statements about who they are in Christ to help them experience the ecstasy of salvation today. Once you have written these statements, I want you to either text, call, or speak to the three people God laid on your heart. Ask the Lord to manifest His joy on you while you share the bliss.

Reflection Questions

After learning more about the definitions of bliss, where do you see bliss in your life?

What does salvation mean to you? How would you explain the ecstasy of salvation to someone else?

DAY 23

FEAST ON HIS PRAYER

Food for Thought: What would happen if the Bride of Christ saw herself as already married?

When Jesus had finished saying all these things he looked up to heaven and said, "Father, the time has come. Reveal the glory of your Son so that he can give the glory back to you."

John 17:1 (TLB)

Jesus' Heart

The entire chapter of John 17 is Jesus praying to the Father. In the very first verse, Jesus asks the Father to reveal His glory so that it can go right back to the Father. I want to pray that same way. Any glory that comes my way, I want to give right back to Jesus! In today's feast we will be savoring portions of Jesus' prayer from John 17. May the aroma of this prayer fill our hearts with Jesus' words so that we, too, can be more like Him.

"Eternal life means to know and experience you as the only true God, and to know and experience Jesus Christ, as the Son whom you have sent."

John 17:3 (TPT)

We are meant to experience God and Jesus, and to know them intimately. That is how we have eternal life. Once we are born again, our eternal life begins here on earth because we enter union with Christ and the Father. Our spiritual birthday is the day we start to experience fellowship with Christ. Imagine it: you get to experience the Lord every day. You don't just learn *about* Him; you live *with* Him.

"My plea is not for the world but for those you have given me because they belong to you. And all of them, since they are mine, belong to you; and you have given them back to me with everything else of yours, and so they are my glory!"

John 17:9-10 (TLB)

You belong to Christ and He gives you a place to belong. He is your home. He took you out of the pit and placed you right next to Himself. He put you in a place where you get to be His glory! Wow. I am Jesus' glory! Marinate on that for a minute until it sinks in.

Often, we can't see ourselves as worth much, but here Jesus is saying you are His glory and that you belong to Him. He prides Himself that you belong to Him. Your very existence gives Him glory. May you feel His deep, deep love for you right now. I recommend you go back to verses 9-10 and read them again.

"And now I am coming to you. I have told them many things while I was with them so that they would be filled with my joy."

John 17:13 (TLB)

Jesus fills you with His joy. As we read the Word and feast on all Jesus said, we should be filled with more of His joy. His joy is supernatural; it is a joy that is not an emotion, but a state of being. His joy is constant. His joy is in you. He never said we would have to complete something to receive His joy. He does it all.

> "I'm not asking that you remove them from this world, but I ask that you guard their hearts from evil."
>
> John 17:15 (TPT)

Jesus specifically prays that the Father will protect us. He did not want us to be taken out of the world. If we were removed from the world, how could we influence it? We are His hands and feet on this earth, and we have Jesus' authority. He gave us this authority so that we can affect our world.

You have the Father protecting you from evil and the Enemy. Let's munch on that for a moment. The Creator of all things is protecting you. Jesus knew that God protected Him, which is why He did not worry about things. This is why Jesus asks the Father to watch over us. With God watching out for us, what do we need to fear?

> "I am not praying for these alone but also for the future believers who will come to me because of the testimony of these. My prayer for all of them is that they will be of one heart and mind, just as you and I are, Father—that just as you are in me and I am in you, so they will be in us, and the world will believe you sent me."
>
> John 17:20-21 (TLB)

These verses tell how Jesus was praying for *all* believers, including you and me. He prayed that all of us would share one heart and mind, just like Jesus and the Father. The Bride is meant to be inside the Father and Jesus. Imagine that you and every other believer are dwelling within God and Christ. You flow in and through God and His Son. This is what Jesus was praying.

We were never meant to be a divided church. How is the world supposed to see the truth when Christ's followers don't keep their focus on

Jesus, but instead focus on all the disagreements within different churches? Jesus prayed that we would be unified as one, just as He is one with the Father. He also said that He and the Father would be *in* us. If we have Jesus and the Father in us, then all the fruit of the Spirit should be evident in the church. Jesus called the collective church—all those who hear the testimony of Christ and believe—His Bride. When believers are united as *one* Bride, the world can truly see Jesus and know that God sent Him.

> "For the very glory you have given to me I have given them so that they will be joined together as one and experience the same unity that we enjoy. You live fully in me and now I live fully in them so they will experience perfect unity, and the world will be convinced that you have sent me, for they will see that you love each one of them with the same passionate love that you have for me."
>
> John 17:22-23 (TPT)

In these verses Jesus is expressing how He gives us His glory. When you encounter the glory of the Lord, it changes you. Jesus is saying that it will bring about a oneness with all those who believe in Him. The glory of the Lord drips with unity because Jesus, the manifestation of God's glory, is the Lord's answer to perfect union with us. Our unity, as believers, is the outward expression of how Christ was unified with the Father.

When we get that glory on us, it shifts the atmosphere to reflect heaven. There is no discord in heaven. With His glory, we get His fullness, His love, His harmony—His intimacy. When we know we are glory carriers, the evidence is all around us. The world sees the glory. It feels the passionate love that God has for all of us.

> "I have revealed to them who you are and I will continue to make you even more real to them so that they may experience the same endless love that you have for me, for your love will now live in them, even as I live in them!"
>
> John 17:26 (TPT)

Jesus tells us in this last verse that He lives in us. Where He lives, love lives. You have the Son of God living in you! You have Love living in you because Jesus is love.

Jesus also tells us here that He is constantly revealing more of the Father. The closer we lean into Jesus, the more we know the mysteries of the Father. One of the mysteries that Jesus reveals is what endless love feels like. Endless love is unconditional, non circumstantial, and without limit.

Throughout this prayer we can see the importance of all the aspects of Jesus we have feasted on for 22 days. Jesus' heart is unveiled in this prayer in John 17. His heart is for you to see yourself in union with Him. He wants you to know that you are special, loved, wrapped in glory, and protected. Fill up at His table; every portion you will find there is connected to His prayer over you.

SNACK TIME!

Intercession

I wanted to include a little snack for us before dessert. Let's enjoy some truths about intercession. Jesus is our Intercessor who sits at the right hand of God (Romans 8:34). Jesus fulfilled the Levitical role and is now our High Priest. He constantly intercedes on our behalf (Hebrews 7:25). To be an intercessor is to speak with God on someone or something's behalf. We must always be ready to come before God and ask for solutions.

I love being with intercessors who come together and align their hearts with Jesus. The intercession room is filled with one thought: what/who does Jesus want us to intercede for today? As we pray in the Spirit and listen, suddenly the room is filled with His presence, and people start praying for whatever is placed on their heart. Christ cares for all things and all issues. He wants us to unite with Him and pray against injustice, corruption, etc. We are to pray for healing, our communities, our government, the world, and more.

Interceding is standing in the gap so that problems can be reconciled. Jesus stands for us as the Intercessor who reconciled us to God and is always there for us.

> "My children, I am writing these things to you so that you will not sin. But if anyone does sin, we have an Intercessor with the Father—the righteous Messiah Yeshua."
>
> 1 John 2:1 (TLV)

Prayer Nutrition Label

Nutrition Facts

Unlimited servings per container

Serving size   **Overflowing cups**

Amount per serving

Christe

Consumption is a great source for the following: **% Daily Value***

Experiencing eternal life now	100%
Knowing you belong to Jesus	100%
Being protected by the Ultimate One	100%
Coming into unity with all believers	100%
Living fully in God and the Son	100%
Flowing in endless love	100%

*The % Daily Value (DV) tells you how much a nutrient in a serving contributes to a daily diet. Feasting on His Prayer every day is recommended for heavenly nutritional health.

DESSERT

Daily Bread

Today, let's create a dessert by tasting the Lord's Model Prayer first and then making a prayer unique to you. I want you to read Matthew 6:9-13 in your favorite translation. Think about the Lord's prayer.

Reflection Questions

What does Jesus mean with each section of the prayer? Write down your answers.

How can this prayer influence your life now? Write down your thoughts.

Now, sit with the Lord and write out your own short prayer. Pray this prayer for a few days and then write down how you feel. How did your mind shift this week?

DAY 24

FEAST ON HIS COMPASSION

Food for Thought: When you look at people, do you spend more time focusing on the outside or on the inside?

Just as he neared the gate of the town, a dead man was being carried out. He was his mother's only son, and she was a widow. A large crowd from the town was also with her. When the Lord saw her, he had compassion on her and said, "Don't weep." Then he came up and touched the open coffin, and the pallbearers stopped. And he said, "Young man, I tell you, get up!" The dead man sat up and began to speak, and Jesus gave him to his mother.

Luke 7:12-15 (CSB)

Moved to Action

All throughout the Gospels we read how Jesus was moved by compassion to heal the sick, feed the multitude, and teach those who were lost. Since I'm a "wordy" (a person who loves word definitions), I looked into the definition of the word *compassion* from Luke 7:13 in both the dictionary and Thayer's Greek Lexicon.

The Greek word used for compassion in the Gospels is [9]*splagchnizo-mai* which means "to be moved as to one's bowels (for the bowels were thought to be the seat of love and pity)." I don't know about you, but I am intrigued by this definition. Compassion moves us so greatly that the Greek used here refers to how compassion originates from our deepest, innermost places.

In the dictionary [10]*compassion* means that someone is aware of another's distress and wants to relieve that distress. Jesus was constantly conscious of people's pain and sorrow, and He wanted them to be free. When we partake in Jesus' compassion, we must be aware of the world around us and then be moved to do something about it. It is not compassion to watch someone struggle and leave them to work it out on their own. Compassion is putting yourself aside for the sake of someone else.

In Luke 7:12-15 Jesus stops a funeral procession and raises the dead because He felt the sorrow of the widow and wanted to restore her life as well as her son's. Without her son, she had nothing left. Jesus was moved to give them both a future. In Matthew 14:14-21, Jesus is moved with compassion for the multitude. He heals the sick and then feeds them. The disciples wanted the people to be sent away to feed themselves, but Jesus was moved to action. This is why He fed them. In Mark 1:40-42, we see a leper come up to Jesus pleading to be healed. Jesus is moved with compassion and tells the leper He wants to heal him. Jesus touches the leper who is immediately cleansed. Jesus was not just sympathetic with the leper; He changed the leper's life. Compassion is when you are so close in union with Jesus that you begin to feel His heart for those around you. Compassion is supposed to run so deep within us that we are moved to action.

---

9   Sourced from blueletterbible.org (G4697)

10   https://www.merriam-webster.com/dictionary/compassion

See the Gold

I want to share some examples of how feasting on Jesus' compassion allows you to see the gold in others. I have the privilege of going on ministry trips with Global Celebration. On these trips we always get to find the amazing people who live in garbage dumps. I'm going to be honest with you, if you are not moved with compassion, these are not the trips for you. The people live in garbage, which means that we work in filth. We work with the diseased, dirty, and malnourished. However, we bring heaven to the garbage dumps. We look past the outward appearance and see the gold ready to be brought to the surface.

I'll never forget the first time I tried to hug a young woman who lived in the garbage. She leaned back and told me how dirty she was. I told her that I didn't care and hugged her anyway. She was tense at first, but then I slowly felt all her pressure and tension dissolve in my arms. She started to cry, and I just held her. I stroked her hair and told her how much she was loved. English was not her language, but I knew it didn't matter. Hugs pass through any language barrier. I wanted her to know how precious she was as a person. She encountered Jesus that day. Compassion causes us to do things that seem strange to the world and maybe to our own minds. Compassion brings healing. Compassion brings nourishment. Jesus shows us that with His life.

Another time, I was ministering in a garbage dump in Mexico. I saw a young man on top of a mountain of trash. This was a literal mountain of trash, just so you know. I could tell he was standing up there, away from all of us, to isolate himself. I knew I had to talk to him, so I told some of my friends that I was going to climb the mountain. I knew it was dangerous (trash sink holes have killed people), but I was moved strongly by compassion. My friends decided to join me! (I love the kingdom. God brings people together who share the same heart.) We worked our way up the mountain.

About halfway up we encountered a man who was sick with severe stomach pain. He was shocked to see us up on the mountain and warned us that it was dangerous, but we told him that we came to spend time with him and others on the mountain. We were with him for a while and then prayed for him to be healed. After praying for his healing, we continued climbing and finally reached the secluded young man. He was completely shocked to see us up there. He kept his distance at first, but it didn't take long for us to build rapport. My friend was even able to hug and pray for him. We had a little love ambush on top of a trash mountain with this young man. He even smiled and hugged us all goodbye when it was time to leave. The next day, the man we had prayed for to be healed from severe stomach pain came up to me. He had been completely healed the night before. He then brought us other people and asked that we pray for their healing as well!

We need to partake in Jesus' compassion. The world needs you and me to demonstrate compassion as Jesus did. We need His compassion to settle inside of us, in our bowels. We need to reach those who seem unreachable. We need to love those who have been labeled as unlovable. We need to free people who have been in bondage for so long. Jesus traveled, preached the good news, and healed the sick. He calls us to share His compassion because the world needs us. The Bible tells us that the harvest is great, but the workers are few. If we don't go, who will?

And what pity he felt for the crowds that came, because their problems were so great and they didn't know what to do or where to go for help. They were like sheep without a shepherd. "The harvest is so great, and the workers are so few," he told his disciples. "So pray to the one in charge of the harvesting, and ask him to recruit more workers for his harvest fields."

Matthew 9:36-38 (TLB)

The compassion that Jesus shares with us is easy to access. His heart beats in you. He shares His thoughts with you. Just be ready and willing to act on His promptings.

Compassion Nutrition Label

Nutrition Facts

Unlimited servings per container

Serving size   **Overflowing cups**

Amount per serving

Christ

Consumption is a great source for the following: **% Daily Value***

Showing compassion with action	100%
Seeing "the gold" in people	100%
Feeling Jesus' heartbeat	100%
Being a harvester	100%
Restoring lives and changing hearts	100%
Getting excited to go to garbage dumps	100%

*The % Daily Value (DV) tells you how much a nutrient in a serving contributes to a daily diet. Feasting on His Compassion every day is recommended for heavenly nutritional health.

DESSERT

Demonstrate Compassion

The definition of compassion is to be aware of other's distress and then help relieve it. Keep a lookout for people in distress this week. It could be a friend, family member, stranger, or co-worker. You can even find a way to demonstrate compassion during your church's ministry time. Ask the Lord to show you how you can help someone in distress. He will tell you exactly what to do and say if you ask and then listen to Him.

Active Listening

One way that helps me demonstrate compassion is with active listening. To help people, we need to know what is going on, and the more information we have, the more we can ask the Holy Spirit how we should act. Active listening is removing all distractions to focus on what the speaker is saying. The speaker must feel like they are being listened to, and the listener must be able to demonstrate that they did, in fact, listen. Here are some tips for active listening.

1. Remove external distractions.
    » Turn off your phone and other electronics with notifications.
    » Turn off music or other noises that would grab your attention.

2. Remove internal distractions.
   - » Stop thinking about things you need or want to do and clear your mind.
   - » Focus only on the person speaking.

3. Make eye contact.
   - » Make sure to look at the speaker.
   - » Taking notes requires a lot of looking down, which can make a person feel like you are not paying attention. Be mindful of this and make eye contact most of the time.
   - » If you are listening on the phone, give verbal acknowledgments that you are listening. For example: The speaker says something and then you could say, "That's a great point." Make a simple statement to let them know you are listening, but do not redirect the conversation to yourself.

4. Keep your body language open and inviting.
   - » Avoid crossing your arms or tapping your foot. This can seem like you are impatient and want the speaker to hurry up.

5. Summarize what the speaker is saying.
   - » Use simple statements to sum up what you heard so the speaker feels like you did pay attention. This will also allow the speaker to correct you if you misunderstood something.

Reminder: Take a moment and drink in His New Wine with this feast

DAY 25

FEAST ON HIS WISDOM

> **Food for Thought:** "I am not afraid of an army of lions led by a sheep; I am afraid of an army of sheep led by a lion." — Alexander the Great

The fear of the Lord is the beginning of knowledge; Fools despise wisdom and instruction.

Proverbs 1:7 (NASB)

Attributes of Wisdom

Do you want your life to be full of vitality, joy, riches, health, and peace? If so, you need wisdom. There was a reason why Solomon was so greatly blessed when he asked God for wisdom (1 Kings 3). Wisdom is how we gain supernatural understanding and revelations from heaven. Solomon could solve problems and give counsel in ways no one else could. People traveled from all over to hear Solomon's wisdom (1 Kings 4).

What does this wisdom look like?

> But the wisdom that comes from heaven is first of all pure and full of quiet gentleness. Then it is peace-loving and courteous. It allows

discussion and is willing to yield to others; it is full of mercy and good deeds. It is wholehearted and straightforward and sincere.

James 3:17 (TLB)

God's wisdom is gentle, solves problems, is full of goodness, and has integrity. God's wisdom does not result in corruption, loss, or deception. His wisdom will leave a situation better than it was before. This wisdom is not just for business or ministry. Wisdom is meant for every part of your life. Proverbs 24:14 says, "Know that [skillful and godly] wisdom is [so very good] for your life and soul; If you find wisdom, then there will be a *future* and a *reward*, and your hope and expectation will not be cut off" (AMP, italics added for emphasis). If you want God's wisdom, ask Him! Whenever you have a decision to make, ask Him about it. Whenever there is a problem that doesn't seem to have a solution, ask Him about it! There is nothing that God's wisdom cannot fix.

My life verse since I was a little girl is Proverbs 3:5-6: "Trust God from the bottom of your heart; don't try to figure out everything on your own. Listen for God's voice in everything you do, everywhere you go; he's the one who will keep you on track" (MSG). I don't have all the answers, but God does. I don't want to make the wrong choices with my life, and I don't have to worry about that. God won't let me miss the destiny He has for me when I lean on Him.

These verses remind me that God will give me His wisdom to make choices that lead me where He wants me to go. The same is true for you. Get into your prayer room and change it to a listening room. He will speak to you. He wants to give you His wisdom because He wants His people to be wise. The world may define wisdom one way, but God's wisdom results in heaven manifesting here on earth. The world needs heavenly wisdom because that is how the earth starts to look more like heaven. His wisdom will always put people first and foremost—not money, not power, not the most logical solution—people. The more we drink in His wisdom, the more we can influence the world around us.

The Influence of Wisdom

In Proverbs 8 wisdom is personified so that we as readers can see the character and influence of wisdom. This character of wisdom is God and His Son because Jesus became wisdom to us (1 Corinthains 1:30). Proverbs 8:6 says, "The meaning of my words will release within you revelation for you to reign in life. My lyrics will empower you to live by what is right" (TPT). We are called to influence the world around us, and wisdom is how we know what to do and when to do it.

We need revelations of wisdom to sit in places of authority. Proverbs 8:11 says, "Wisdom is so priceless that it exceeds the value of any jewel. Nothing you could wish for can equal her" (TPT). I love this verse because it basically means that possessing all the money in the world cannot compare to possessing wisdom. If you have wisdom, riches and honor will follow (Proverbs 3:16). "You will find true success when you find me, for I have insight into wise plans that are designed just for you. I hold in my hands living-understanding, courage, and strength. I empower kings to reign and rulers to make laws that are just" (Proverbs 8:14-15, TPT).

God has a plan just for you. No one else can do what He has made you to do. His wisdom will give you everything you need to see His plan accomplished. Right now, I pray that you will be empowered to believe that you are an influence in this world—that you have a special calling.

How do we see the influence of wisdom in our lives? We seek the Lord's wisdom with our hearts. This goes back to not just studying the Word but eating it. Many popular life principles come from the book of Proverbs, such as "iron sharpens iron" (Proverbs 27:17) or that the wise think before they act (Proverbs 13:16). The Bible is filled with wisdom that is applicable to all areas of our lives.

Right before I got married, my dad came to me and informed me he had some advice for a happy marriage. He told me that no matter what happens in a day, I should never go to sleep angry with my husband.

This nugget of wisdom my dad shared with me is found in Ephesians 4:26-27. These verses tell us not to let the sun set on our anger so that we do not give the devil an opportunity. Unresolved anger can destroy relationships. This word of wisdom has saved James and I countless times from letting resentment and bitterness seep into our marriage. No matter what happens, we talk it out before going to sleep. Even after almost 18 years of marriage, we only go to sleep when there is peace between us. God's Word is living wisdom. Reflect and act on His words. You will start to see wisdom's influence in your life. I guarantee it!

I want to mention one more thing during this wisdom feast. Proverbs 8:16 mentions that Wisdom empowers kings to reign. We are called to reign with Christ (2 Timothy 2:12). Doesn't this make us kings and queens? If we are kings and queens, then we have the position and authority to unravel some of the mysteries of God. Romans 11:33 tells us, "We cannot wrap our minds around God's wisdom and knowledge! Its depths can never be measured! We cannot understand His judgments or explain the mysterious ways that He works!" (VOICE). We will never be able to know or understand everything about God, but Proverbs 25:2 says, "It is the glory of God to conceal a matter, But the glory of kings is to search out a matter" (NASB). When we encounter situations that seem to have no obvious answer or solution, it is our opportunity to glorify God by seeking out His wisdom for answers.

Through Christ we are completely changed from being common to being kingly. We need to stop living like we are common and live like we are royalty. Let His wisdom run through your veins. Let it flow through your heart and into your mind. I often pray for my mind to be renewed with His wisdom. I pray this for you as well.

As we consume more of His wisdom, let us share our discoveries with one another. As we unfold His mysteries, we need to share them with each other. This is how we encourage and strengthen the Bride of Christ. Here is one final verse for you to feast on: "Let the message about Christ, in all its richness, fill your lives. Teach and counsel each other with all the wisdom he gives. Sing psalms and hymns and spiritual songs to God with thankful hearts" (Colossians 3:16, NLT).

Wisdom Nutrition Label

Nutrition Facts

Unlimited servings per container

Serving size   **Overflowing cups**

Amount per serving

Christ

Consumption is a great source for

the following: % Daily Value*

Accessing riches and honor	100%
Trusting God to lead you	100%
Being an influence for heaven	100%
Knowing you have something priceless	100%
Searching out God's mysteries	100%
Living in a state of constant learning	100%

*The % Daily Value (DV) tells you how much a nutrient in a serving contributes to a daily diet. Feasting on His Wisdom every day is recommended for heavenly nutritional health.

DESSERT

Food for the Wise

In Proverbs 9 we are invited to Wisdom's feast. Verse 4 says, "Whoever wants to know me and receive my wisdom, come and dine at my table and drink of my wine" (TPT). We dine and drink through intimacy with the Lord. Spend time with the Lord in a listening room today. Write down what you hear Him say to you. Afterwards, look through His Word and write down 2-3 wisdom nuggets that you can chew on all week. However, I don't want you to stop at chewing on them. I want you to swallow them and let their nutrients affect your life.

Reflection Questions

Where do you see yourself apply God's wisdom in your relationships?

In what areas do you want more of God's wisdom? Write them down and then pray for God to give you His wisdom in those areas.

Holy Spirit Spice Bomb:

You are not defined by your mistakes. You
are defined by Jesus' perfection.

SOUP DU JOUR

Jewish Wedding Soup

Made with Israeli Lamb, heavenly herbs, Holy Spirit spices, and promise-fulfilling pasta

Includes Bread of Life for dipping

*Recommendation: a glass of New Wine to enhance all the flavors

DAY 26

FEAST ON HIS KINGDOM

Food for Thought: If faith like a mustard seed can move mountains, what could faith like Jesus' move?

Jesus, grilled by the Pharisees on when the kingdom of God would come, answered, "The kingdom of God doesn't come by counting the days on the calendar. Nor when someone says, 'Look here!' or, 'There it is!' And why? Because God's kingdom is already among you."

Luke 17:20-21 (MSG)

The Gospel of the Kingdom

Jesus preached the gospel of the kingdom everywhere He went. "Jesus was going through all the cities and villages, teaching in their synagogues and proclaiming the gospel of the kingdom, and healing every disease and every sickness" (Mathew 9:35, NASB). His gospel was filled with good news about repentance, redemption, joy, abundance, freedom, peace, and more. All our meal plans so far have consisted of portions of the kingdom of God.

One of the amazing things about Jesus is that He didn't just preach the kingdom, He demonstrated it. In John 10:37-38 Jesus told the people around Him that they did not have to believe Him if He did not do the works of the Father. The works that Jesus carried out demonstrated His union with the Father. These works consisted of healings, miracles, and restoration. Jesus knew that the people needed to see the power of what He was preaching. 1 Corinthians 4:20 says, "For the Kingdom of God is not a matter of words but of power" (GNT). For too long, the Israelites had been listening to a gospel that was based on man's effort instead of God's love, power, and grace. Jesus' gospel was true life, not a band-aid to "just get by" in life. This is why He healed all who came to Him, cast out demons, and raised the dead. He wanted people to see the power of God and how much He cared for them. Jesus demonstrated what a free life—a life restored to God—could be like. His gospel was displaying God's will for all to see through power. His gospel clearly showed God's heart to be united with humanity, and He empowers us to demonstrate the same gospel.

In Matthew 5:3-10 (NASB), Jesus preached the Sermon on the Mount, which showcased the qualities of His kingdom.

> "Blessed are the poor in spirit, for theirs is the kingdom of heaven" (verse 3).

Humility is how we enter His kingdom. We must fully understand how much we need God (and God alone) to receive life.

> "Blessed are those who mourn, for they will be comforted" (verse 4).

We do not cry and mourn as those with no hope. The kingdom gives us everlasting comfort because we have a hope in Jesus.

> "Blessed are the gentle, for they will inherit the earth" (verse 5).

God is calling us to have a heart like Him. His heart is tender and loving. We are meant to inherit the earth, so we need to share in His gentleness.

"Blessed are those who hunger and thirst for righteousness, for they will be satisfied" (verse 6).

Many have strived since the fall of Adam and Eve to be considered clean and justified before God. In God's kingdom we receive our righteousness through Jesus, which grants us access to His throne room.

"Blessed are the merciful, for they will receive mercy" (verse 7).

God lavishly showers us with His mercy. We must follow His actions and be merciful towards others.

"Blessed are the pure in heart, for they will see God" (verse 8).

There is no sin and corruption in God's kingdom. He has purified us so that we can be united with Him.

"Blessed are the peacemakers, for they will be called sons of God" (verse 9).

The kingdoms of this world cause chaos. God calls us to be His peacemakers so that people will see His kingdom in action now.

"Blessed are those who have been persecuted for the sake of righteousness, for theirs is the kingdom of heaven" (verse 10).

Jesus did not fit into this world and neither do we. God's people should stand out as lights against the darkness. When we get persecuted for standing up for His righteousness, we can always remember that His kingdom is greater than all the kingdoms of this world. Remember, your rightful place is in His kingdom.

Jesus commissioned us to go into all the world and preach the gospel of His kingdom. This means that everywhere we go, we bring His kingdom to earth and showcase what it looks like for all to see—just like He did.

Carry the Kingdom

Jesus describes the kingdom of heaven in many different ways in the Bible. In Matthew 13:44 He compares it to a treasure that was hidden in a field. The one who found it sells everything with joy to buy the field to possess the treasure. He also compares the kingdom to a fine pearl (Matthew 13:45-46). When the merchant finds it, he sells everything and buys the pearl.

Gaining access to the kingdom of God is worth everything. It is priceless. Why? Because living in the kingdom of God is an invitation to live a supernatural life, filled with all the promises and resources of God. Living in the kingdom is living *with* God!

I used to think that I had to wait to see the kingdom of God. I would faithfully pray "thy kingdom come." Then one day, the Lord said to me, "You carry My kingdom. Your heart beats with that prayer, and I answer it everywhere you go." I was overwhelmed at the thought that I can carry His kingdom now! I can carry it everywhere I go. I can see His kingdom manifest around me. I can bring His kingdom to all those who are lost and suffering. I have no special platform or title, no fortune or large influence, but God has entrusted me with His kingdom!

I started to read the Bible with what seemed like new eyes. I read how Jesus carried the kingdom everywhere He went. He even told the Pharisees, "But if I cast out the demons by the Spirit of God, then the kingdom of God has come upon you" (Matthew 12:28, NASB). I never realized while reading the Word that Jesus was displaying the realities of the kingdom of God back then, which is what He calls us to do today. "He said, 'The time has come, and God's kingdom is near. Change the way you think and act, and believe the Good News'" (Mark 1:15, GW). If God's kingdom is near, that means it is close enough to grab hold of and take with you.

Even the apostles carried the kingdom. They showcased what Jesus meant in Matthew 13:31-32.

> Jesus told them another parable: "The Kingdom of heaven is like this. A man takes a mustard seed and sows it in his field. It is the smallest of all seeds, but when it grows up, it is the biggest of all

plants. It becomes a tree, so that birds come and make their nests in its branches" (GNT).

The apostles spoke about the kingdom of heaven everywhere they went. Their words were planted in cities and became churches, which in turn carried the kingdom to more places. We are called to take this gospel of the kingdom, not just speak about it but show the world what it looks like. We carry the kingdom inside of us because the kingdom is where Jesus resides. He resides in us. He is how we manifest the kingdom of heaven here on earth. The world is waiting for us to carry it, plant it, and then watch as it continues to spread to the furthest reaches of the earth.

I like to imagine that I am carrying out invitations to the greatest feast of joy and love that will ever exist. Feasting *on* His kingdom is much like feasting *in* His kingdom. Everything is about Jesus and what He has done for us and to us!

Kingdom Nutrition Label

Nutrition Facts

Unlimited servings per container

Serving size   **Overflowing cups**

Amount per serving

Christment

Consumption is a great source for the following: **% Daily Value***

Recognizing our positions of authority	100%
Stepping into our inheritance	100%
Being able to access the King 24/7	100%
Increasing the domain of heaven	100%
Demonstrating kingdom life	100%
Inviting others to come join the feast	100%

*The % Daily Value (DV) tells you how much a nutrient in a serving contributes to a daily diet. Feasting on His Kingdom every day is recommended for heavenly nutritional health.

DESSERT

Power Punch—Better than Fruit Punch

In the kingdom of God, we get to drink in His power. The world will know that Jesus is in us because we will do the works that He did. Jesus promised us that the Holy Spirit would give us power (Luke 1:35). This means that you have the power of God within you. We are not powerless in the face of the Enemy. We are powerful and can completely disrupt the plans of the Enemy. Let's drink some Power Punch. Say these statements out loud:

- I have Jesus' power to heal the sick.
- I have Jesus' power to cast out demons.
- I have Jesus' power to raise the dead.
- I have Jesus' power to set the captives free.
- I have access to all the resources in the kingdom of God today.
- I have Jesus' power to ignite revival.
- I have Jesus' power to restore the broken.
- I have Jesus' power flowing within me.
- I have Jesus' power to share and demonstrate the good news.

Mustard Seeds

Once you toast mustard seeds, they start to unleash their flavor. For something so small, they can disperse a ton of flavor into whatever you are using them to make. Today, let's imagine that you are like that mustard seed. Even though you may seem small, you pack a ton of power. It is now time to recognize that everything you do has the ability to influence the flavors around you. Where do you see yourself as having the greatest influence right now? How are you influencing? Where would you like to have more influence? Why? Use your answers to ask God for increase.

DAY 27

FEAST ON HIS AUTHORITY

> **Food for Thought:** If the Chef gives you the recipe, He gives you the authority to recreate it.

I will give you the keys *(authority)* of the kingdom of heaven; and whatever you bind [forbid, declare to be improper and unlawful] on earth will have [already] been bound in heaven, and whatever you loose [permit, declare lawful] on earth will have [already] been loosed in heaven.

Matthew 16:19 (AMP, italics added for emphasis)

Dominion

During yesterday's meal we chewed on how the kingdom of God is shown through power. The power of the kingdom of heaven on earth is the authority of Christ in us. I placed today's meal directly after "Feasting on His Kingdom" because I want us to understand something. Jesus has already established His kingdom; He has already restored us to be able to live as God designed. His design has always included intimacy, favor, and co-reigning.

From the beginning God gave dominion over the earth to mankind. Genesis 1:28 says, "Then God blessed them, and God said to them, 'Be fruitful and multiply; fill the earth and *subdue* it; have *dominion* over the fish of the sea, over the birds of the air, and over every living thing that moves on the earth'" (NKJV, italics added for emphasis). This word "dominion" means to rule and to dominate (Strongs [11]H7287). God's intent was not for us to be enslaved by the kingdoms of this world but to increase the kingdom of heaven on this earth. How do we do that? By expanding heaven's territory here on earth.

Once Christ freed us, sin no longer held dominion over us (Romans 6:14). We were transferred from the domain of darkness into the kingdom of Jesus (Colossians 1:13). This means that our authority to subdue the earth was restored. Since we are a part of a different kingdom now, we have the authority to represent that kingdom. We are Christ's ambassadors (2 Corinthains 5:20). Ambassadors are special because they represent their government (kingdom) everywhere they go.

This is why Matthew 16:19 (our verse of the day) is so important for us. Jesus gave us the authority of His kingdom to establish a new spiritual law and order here on earth. This new law and order is directly tied to heaven, so that what we prohibit (bind, chain) here on earth is already prohibited in heaven. What we allow (permit, loose) on earth is already allowed in heaven.

Keep this in mind when you go to your office, school, hospital, etc. Ambassadors are supposed to take heaven into their sphere of influence, whether it is related to media, ministry, health, government, family, entertainment, or education. The more time we spend in the light at His table, the more we recognize how the domain of darkness has been influencing these arenas.

It is time that we recognized the power and position we have in Christ, so we can take back dominion. "I've given you true authority. You can

---

smash vipers and scorpions under your feet. You can walk all over the power of the enemy. You can't be harmed" (Luke 10:19, VOICE). Let's stop playing defense and go on the offensive. We have true authority from Christ to keep the Enemy under our feet.

People of Authority

In Matthew 8:5-13 we can read the story of the centurion officer asking Jesus to heal his servant. Jesus tells the officer that He will come.

> But the centurion replied, "Lord, I am not worthy for You to come under my roof, but just say the word, and my servant will be healed. For I also am a man *under authority*, with soldiers under me; and I say to this one, 'Go!' and he goes, and to another, 'Come!' and he comes, and to my slave, 'Do this!' and he does it."
>
> Matthew 8:8-9 (NASB, italics added for emphasis).

This officer recognized authority and believed Jesus would heal his servant because Jesus said He would. What if we looked in the mirror and recognized authority? What if we were so united with Jesus that the spirits of affliction and disease left the sick when our shadows passed by? This is my heart's desire. The closer I grow to Jesus, the more I grow in my Christ-given authority.

Authority is tied to intimacy. The closer we draw to our Bridegroom, we start to look and sound like Him. The Enemy is not dumb. He recognizes those who operate in authority and those who do not. This is why we do not have to play with demons or allow them to put on a show in our presence. Demons like to be dramatic. They like to scare believers by growling, climbing up walls, throwing up, or screaming. However, once a word spoken with authority is released, all the parlor tricks cease, and the demon flees.

When I'm out on the streets, in the drug parks, or in a garbage dump, I want the people who come with me not just to know they have authority but believe it and demonstrate it. I often find myself in places where there is a lot of darkness because I am called to carry the light. I could not be the light if I didn't understand that my brightness is far greater than their darkness. "Then Jesus again spoke to them, saying, 'I am the Light of the world; the one who follows Me will not walk in the darkness, but will have the Light of life'" (John 8:12, NASB). We are people who have the Light of life in us!

We are people of authority because the One who was given all authority gave us our mission. Mark 16:15-18 says,

> Then Jesus said to them, "So wherever you go in the world, tell everyone the Good News. Whoever believes and is baptized will be saved, but whoever does not believe will be condemned. These are the miraculous signs that will accompany believers: They will use the *power* and *authority* of my name to force demons out of people. They will speak new languages. They will pick up snakes, and if they drink any deadly poison, it will not hurt them. They will place their hands on the sick and cure them" (GW, italics added for emphasis).

These are our orders as ambassadors. Jesus told us to operate in the power and authority of His name. Our orders were never supposed to be optional. We are supposed to share the good news, cast out demons, walk in protection, and heal the sick. It is time we are recognized as people of authority everywhere we go.

This is why we feast on His authority. We need it to be so substantial inside of us that even the forces of darkness tremble when we walk in. I think of it like this: sometimes we can tell what someone has been feasting on because the aroma comes out of their pores. I want Jesus, His power, His authority, and His love to come out of my pores. Let's consume so much of Him that He diffuses into the environment around us, including all of our spheres of influence.

Authority Nutrition Label

Nutrition Facts

Unlimited servings per container

Serving size   **Overflowing cups**

Amount per serving

Christy

Consumption is a great source

for the following: % Daily Value*

Living as an ambassador for Christ	100%
Bringing heaven's law and order here	100%
Influencing all the world's arenas	100%
Recognizing your power in Christ	100%
Diffusing Christ's aroma around you	100%
Causing the Enemy to tremble	100%

*The % Daily Value (DV) tells you how much a nutrient in a serving contributes to a daily diet. Feasting on His Authority every day is recommended for heavenly nutritional health.

DESSERT

Prophetic Snack Activation

For today's dessert I would recommend you get 2-3 friends to participate. You need to get your favorite snack. If you can be with your friends
in person, tell them to bring their favorite snack. If you cannot, send a
picture of your favorite snack to each other. Ask the Lord to give you a
prophetic word about your friends' snacks. For example: My friend loves
grapes. So, the Lord highlights the fact that there was a bunch of grapes
all nestled together. I then give my friend a prophetic word about being
nestled together in a likeminded community. Have fun with this dessert.
It is designed to activate your awareness of how God speaks to you in
different ways.

Reflection Questions

Describe what being an ambassador for Christ looks and sounds like
to you.

Describe a time when the authority of Jesus flowed out of you. What
happened? Why do you think it flowed out at that time?

DAY 28

FEAST ON HIS ABUNDANCE

Food for Thought: Do you plan for lack or do you plan for abundance?

The thief comes only in order to steal and kill and destroy. I came that they may have and *enjoy life*, and have it in abundance *[to the full, till it overflows]*.

John 10:10 (AMP, italics added for emphasis)

The Source

Today is the day we get to feast on His abundance! What does this look like? It looks like God pouring so much life into you that you overflow! You don't just have "enough," you have too much to hold. It's like sitting at a table where the food just keeps coming, with more and more richness—quantity and quality that can never be contained. There is just too much goodness for any one person to bask in. The amazing thing about God giving us too much is that this abundant life will overflow out of us and into those around us. Abundance means we get to position ourselves to give, even as we receive.

I'm going to be honest with you. For most of my adult life, I have struggled with worrying about finances. We always had what we needed, but when unexpected bills came, I would get anxious and stressed out. Let me emphasize one thing: worrying does not promote a generous mindset. One day, I was at my desk, looking at one of those unexpected bills and I heard the Lord say, "I'm responsible for you and your family." It took me a moment for those words to sink in. I have always been the main "bread winner" for my family, so I have always shouldered the burden of responsibility. Now, here the Lord is telling me that I didn't have to carry this burden—that I just needed to trust Him to do what His Word says He will do.

I was drawn to Matthew 6:25-34, where Jesus tells us that if God provides food for the birds and clothes for the lilies, why should we worry about it for ourselves? We are so much more valuable to God than birds and lilies. God's Word says that He will meet our needs, so why would I keep begging Him for something that He is already doing? Matthew 6:33 says, "Instead, desire first and foremost God's kingdom and God's righteousness, and all these things will be given to you as well" (CEB). Intimacy with God opens our eyes to see Him as the source of all we need. He is always faithful to provide. Being equipped with this knowledge frees us to jump into the river of generosity.

Many Christians today struggle with finances. They wonder how they will put food on the table or pay the rent. Their experiences cause them to think that they are deficient in some way. "I'm struggling to survive so I must be missing something." It also creates a mindset that says, "I am the source of my provision because if I don't do it, it won't happen." This is not what the Word says.

God is *the* Source. He is *the* Provider. He will supply *all* your needs (Philippians 4:19). Living in abundance is recognizing God as your source. It is also understanding that He has adopted you as a son or daughter. We don't have to worry about asking for things that God already provides as a good Father. My kids don't have to go into the kitchen and beg me for food. They know there is food in the refrigerator. It is the same with God. He has His refrigerator constantly stocked. We get to open it and take what we need. It is time we as believers stop planning for our lack and start planning for God's abundance.

I know that when God tells me to give something, He is faithful to provide. I get to be generous, just like Jesus! I don't know how many times God has told us to give our time, money, and talents to different people and ministries; and because we listened, we were blessed to see God change lives in so many ways.

Generosity is not about *what* you give but *how* you give. It's a heart condition. Jesus even explains this to His disciples in Mark 12 with the story of the widow who gave all she had. She didn't give much in terms of quantity, but she gave the best in terms of quality. Being generous is investing in people and their God-given dreams. We get to partner in advancing God's kingdom with our generosity.

You might ask yourself, what if I don't have the money to give? I used to ask this question to myself all the time. Give anyway if that is what God is telling you.

Let me share a visual example of abundance and generosity. Imagine that you are a hose. God starts running water through you, but then you block the water from going out. You are afraid that there won't be enough if you continue to pour out. God can no longer put more water into you because there is nowhere for the excess to go. You have enough to be full, but you will not be able to water others. You limited the flow. Now imagine that you do not block the water from running out of you. The flow remains constant, and you see that no matter how much water gets released, there will always be more water that continues to fill you up. The flow is limitless. You are now not just full, but abundant, because you are affecting all those around you.

I said it before, and I'll say it again: God doesn't want you to have enough to just get by. He wants you to have too much. He wants you to trust Him, lean on Him, and believe that He came to give you not just life, but an abundant life. How do you do this? Believe that He is the source of all the water you will ever need to flourish in life. Your needs are provided for. Let those worries go. He wants you to keep your eyes on Him and believe that you are designed to live an outrageously abundant life today!

The God of Too Much

Now that we have tasted that God is the Source for all we need, let's take a look at and savor some of the "too much" Bible stories. In Mark 8, Jesus had a multitude of people following Him for three days, with nothing to eat. They were so moved by His teachings that they didn't want to leave Him. Jesus felt compassion for them and wanted to make sure they were fed. Jesus knew that there is limitless abundance in heaven, so He brought that abundance to earth by multiplying food right then and there. Jesus did not focus on the limits in the natural realm where there were only seven loaves of bread and a few fish. He reached into the spirit realm, where there is a never-ending supply, and brought it to the natural realm. How did this story end? With leftovers. They had too much food!

In Matthew 14 Jesus again multiplied food, but this time for more people and with less food to begin with. He only had five loaves and two fish. This story ended with leftovers too, but with more leftovers! The best feasts are the ones where there is too much food, even after everyone has had their fill—just like the feast we get to partake in every day at His table!

Now let's look at a "too many" story. In Genesis 15:5 God told Abraham to go outside, look at the sky, and count the stars. He said that Abraham's descendants would be that numerous. There were too many stars to count! God promised that He would give Abraham more than he could even imagine. God's promise to us is the same. Ephesians 3:20-21 says, "Now to Him who is able to do *far more abundantly* beyond all that we ask or think, according to the power that works within us, to Him be the glory in the church and in Christ Jesus to all generations forever and ever. Amen" (NASB, italics added for emphasis).

The closer you get to Jesus, the more you learn that He loves to give far greater than merely what we need. He loves to give us too much, because then we are equipped to go and give it to others so that they too might live an extravagantly abundant life!

Abundance Nutrition Label

Nutrition Facts

Unlimited servings per container

Serving size   **Overflowing cups**

Amount per serving

Christ   ∞

Consumption is a great source for

the following: **% Daily Value***

Believing God is your source	100%
Removing the "I'm lacking" mindset	100%
Releasing responsibility to Jesus	100%
Being a hose with no blockages	100%
Living in the "too much"	100%
Generously giving to others	100%

***The % Daily Value (DV) tells you how much a nutrient in a serving contributes to a daily diet. Feasting on His Abundance every day is recommended for heavenly nutritional health.**

DESSERT

Voice Activated

For today's dessert I want us to understand the power of our voice. There are so many things in today's world that are voice-activated. Automated devices and systems only need your voice prompts to turn on, fulfill requests, or research information. God was the first to use voice activation in Genesis 1. He spoke all things into existence! Imagine how our lives could change if we realized that when we speak, heaven manifests, miracles happen, and mindsets shift!

Today I want you to do some voice activation. I want you to speak abundance into different areas of your life. Remember Proverbs 18:21 tells us that life and death are in the tongue. This means that you can speak abundant life into existence! Here are some recommendations of areas you can voice-activate: family, friends, relationships, work, school, ministry, health, finances, and creativity.

Reflection Questions

Do you see yourself as an open hose or a closed one from the example in today's meal? Be honest. How can you be more open to let the Lord flow through you in generosity?

Where do you see the God of "too much" in your life? This is where you see Him in outrageous abundance in any area of your life. Share your answer with a friend to testify to God's goodness.

DAY 29

FEAST ON HIS NAME

> **Food for Thought:** If you want an invitation to the wedding feast, get to know the Bridegroom.

That is why God has now lifted him so high, and has given him the name beyond all names, so that at the name of Jesus "every knee shall bow", whether in Heaven or earth or under the earth. And that is why, in the end, "every tongue shall confess" that Jesus Christ" is the Lord, to the glory of God the Father.

Philippians 2:9-10 (PHILLIPS)

The Qualities of God

Today's feast is going to look a little different. I have prepared some of the names of the Lord for us. As you read these names, I want you to savor them. Don't be in a rush. As you taste each one, relish it; let the meanings sink into your being. This is the One who loves you. His names have so much power. We are identified by our names. The qualities of God are also identifiable by His names. I pray that you will intimately know and see each and every quality of God in your life. I pray that this meal leaves you with a glorious aftertaste.

The Creator — (Genesis 1; John 1:3): The One who created all things for good, out of unconditional love.

El-Shaddai — *God Almighty* (Genesis 17:1): The One who holds all power and might to work everything in existence for His glory.

El Roi — *God who sees* (Genesis 16:13): The One who sees all things and cares deeply for every detail in our lives.

Yahweh Kanna — *Jealous God* (Exodus 34:14): The One who is jealous for pure adoration, love, and union.

Yahweh Qadosh — *The Holy One* (Isaiah 40:25): The One who is sacred, perfect, spotless, and incorruptible.

Yahweh Rapha — *God the Healer* (1 Peter 2:24; Exodus 15:26; many more): The One who destroyed *all* sickness and afflictions by His blood.

Ancient of Days — (Daniel 7): The One who sits outside of time.

Everlasting Father — (Isaiah 9:6): The One who protects, loves, provides, and bestows an inheritance.

Wonderful Counselor — (Isaiah 9:6): The One who gives wisdom, correction, guidance, and solutions.

Prince of Peace — (Isaiah 9:6): The One who creates in us a peace that surpasses all logic and reasoning.

Son of Man — Representing Jesus' humanity (many references): The One who stepped out of heaven to live a perfect life in human restraints.

Son of God — Representing Jesus' divinity (John 11:27): The One who came from the Father to display His Father's will.

Messiah (Christ) — (John 11:27): The One who was anointed to fulfill all that was promised by way of the prophets of old.

Immanuel — (Matthew 1:23): The One who came to not only dwell with us but *in* us.

Savior — (1 John 4:14): The One who saves all those who believe from sin and death.

The Lamb of God — (John 1:29): The One who poured out His blood as the perfect sacrifice to bring all those who believe into union with the Father.

The Good Shepard — (John 10:11): The One who guides us to places of blessing and keeps us protected from all enemies.

Alpha and Omega — *The Beginning and the End* (Revelation 22:13): The One who holds time in His hands.

Lion of Judah — (Revelation 5:5): The One who has strength and majesty like no other, who has conquered all His enemies.

High Priest — (Hebrews 4:14-16): The One who intercedes for us, cleanses us, and speaks on our behalf.

King of Kings — (1 Timothy 6:15): The One who is above all lords and all kings. There is no one higher.

The Living Word — (John 1:1): The One who is God's Word and became flesh to fulfill God's purpose. The One who now speaks with the breath of God.

Bread of Life — (John 6:35): The One who came down from heaven to provide everlasting life and nourishment.

Light of the World — (John 8:12): The One who brings hope and removes all darkness everywhere He goes.

The Way — (John 14:6): The One who provides the only path to the Father as well as the means to get there.

The Truth — (John 14:6): The One who demonstrates God's nature and the meaning of His words.

The Life — (John 14:6): The One who is the source of eternal life and a life filled with abundance.

The Last Adam — (1 Corinthians 15:45): The One who takes those born in corruption and recreates them in His perfection.

The Vine — (John 15:5): The One to whom we are connected, who is the source of all fruitfulness in our lives.

Rabbi — *Teacher* (Mark 9:5): The One who instructs us and makes sure we grow in the revelations and mysteries of God.

Friend — (John 15:5): The One who tells us He likes us, who calls us His friends.

The I AM — (Exodus 3:14): The One who is self-existent, who is everything we could ever need for all eternity.

Bridegroom — (Luke 5:33-35): The One who takes my hand, gives me His name, and calls me His Bride.

I end this meal with a toast: To the name above every name, may yours be the glory and the honor forever. Amen.

Name Nutrition Label

Nutrition Facts

Unlimited servings per container

Serving size   **Overflowing cups**

Amount per serving

Christ

Consumption is a great source for

the following: % Daily Value*

Getting hit with bliss	100%
Savoring the Name above all names	100%
Sitting in awe of the One	100%
Living in reverence to the One	100%
Basking in His everything	100%
Relishing in the glory of who He is	100%

*The % Daily Value (DV) tells you how much a nutrient in a serving contributes to a daily diet. Feasting on His Name every day is recommended for heavenly nutritional health.

DESSERT

The Bridegroom's Cake

There is a tradition in some parts of America to have a cake specifically designed for the groom. This cake is meant to reflect the groom in some way. For example, my husband loves shrimp, so I made his groom's cake into the shape of a giant shrimp. Yes, these cakes are supposed to be unique, fun, and often crazy.

Today we feasted on the names of the Lord. Now, we are going to think of how we would design *the* Bridegroom's cake. When you think of Jesus, what do you see? How would your cake showcase Him? Add as many details as you can. You can draw it or write down your description.

DAY 30

FEAST ON HIS FULLNESS

Food for Thought: When a meal is good, people can't help but make food noises.

That Christ will live in you as you open the door and invite him in. And I ask him that with both feet planted firmly on love, you'll be able to take in with all followers of Jesus the extravagant dimensions of Christ's love. Reach out and experience the breadth! Test its length! Plumb the depths! Rise to the heights! *Live full lives, full in the fullness of God.*

Ephesians 3:17-19 (MSG, italics added for emphasis)

Live the Full Life

Today is our final feast. During our meals together we have tasted different facets of the Lord. Each facet makes up just a part of His fullness. My wish is that you would consume all that He is! You can feast on all that Jesus is, and watch as it changes you physically, emotionally, and spiritually. Jesus lacks nothing. He *is* fullness. You lack nothing because He makes you full! "For he is the complete fullness of deity living in human form. And our own completeness is now found in him. We are completely filled with God as Christ's fullness overflows within us" (Colossians 2:9-10a, TPT). You are complete! His fullness overflows within you!

So how do we live life accessing all this fullness every day? We keep our eyes on Christ and Him crucified. All these meals point to Jesus' finished work on the cross. All these meals describe what life is like in the fullness of Christ's accomplishments. When we truly grasp that Christ brought us out of sin and into holy union with Him, everything changes. We access unconditional love, joy, health, abundance, eternal life, and so much more now! We carry the kingdom of God, His authority, and His freedom now! We live the supernatural life here on earth now! Our old relationship with sin is over now! We live a life dead to sin and alive to God now!

I hope you have lost weight over these past 30 days. I know the heaviness that comes with striving for perfection, struggling with sin, living to please people, and seeing yourself as lacking. I hope this weight has been lifted off you. Another wonderful thing about this type of feasting is that when you make it your lifestyle, you don't have to worry about putting the weight back on. The more you feast on Him, the more you start to look like Him, sound like Him, think like Him, and be like Him.

Call to Testify

It is funny how we can always tell when someone is obsessed with something. They can't stop thinking or talking about it. I have had many people tell me that I am constantly talking about Jesus and healing. That is absolutely true. I am obsessed with Jesus! He is the One who freed me, so I want to share His freedom with others. He is the One who healed my heart, so I want more hearts to be healed.

When we are liberated, restored, and empowered, we cannot remain silent. It is impossible. It's like we have an internal party going on, and we want to invite everyone to join us! If you have encountered Jesus, you have a testimony. Your life is a story, all about the goodness of God. The good, the bad, and the ugly can all showcase His goodness because He

THE ULTIMATE FEAST · DAY 30

brings you through it all. Don't let anything or anyone stop you from sharing the good news. I share the good news all the time by simply telling people about my life, my kids, my work, and my ministry. See, I am consumed by Jesus, so it is hard not to boast about Him in some way or another. What usually happens after you eat a great meal? You feel full and then you probably testify to how good the food was. We can be so full of Jesus that He just naturally comes up in any conversation.

Here is something you can chew on. Have you ever wondered if God testifies about you to the angels? I have, and I believe He does. Parents boast about their kids. God boasted about His people in the Bible. Why wouldn't He boast about His people today? I tell my kids all the time how proud of them I am. I want them to recognize their worth, so they recognize worth in others. We testify so that the world will know the value of the Lord. Every testament to God's goodness carries His glory further than before. Don't you want to be a glory carrier?

Your Place at His Table

I have just one more morsel to share before we end our meal today. I want you to know that you always have a place at His table. It is a place specifically designed for you, that can never be taken by anyone else. You don't have to work for this seat. You just accept the invitation. At this table you are positioned to share a never-ending supply of Lamb. This Lamb is the only one that can completely fill you up; it can make you feel priceless, spotless, and able to do the impossible. This Lamb will never leave you in lack, rejected, or alone. Every time we sit in our place at the table, we remember all that the Lamb has done for us.

This is why the early church would meet and hold Agape (love) feasts. They came together at a table to fellowship and feast on all that Jesus accomplished. They would also share the good news, which is why the church grew. When Jesus gathered the disciples around the table during Passover, He told them to take the bread and drink the cup in remembrance of Him and His new covenant. Every day, we need to take our place at His table and feast on Him and His fullness. We need to drink in everything that He is so that we understand He is a part of us, on the inside.

I also want you to realize that your place at His table comes with special privileges. You are given a new identity. You are now united with the Bridegroom. You share His name and all the authority that comes with it. You have access to all the treasures in heaven. You gain entry into the throne room, where you can see the King face-to-face. You become a representative of His kingdom and carry it with you for all to see. You catch His joy. Your life becomes a non-stop celebration of Him! The chains that bound you in the natural realm disappear as you walk freely with His Spirit. Your place at His table is where you belong. You have 24/7 entry. The food never runs out or spoils. Jesus Himself prepared the ultimate feast for you. I challenge you to feast on the Lamb every day. Drink in His Spirit every day. Remember, you are what you eat. Let's be just like Jesus.

Fullness Nutrition Label

Nutrition Facts

Unlimited servings per container

Serving size　　　　　**Overflowing cups**

Amount per serving

Christ

Consumption is a great source for

the following:　　　**% Daily Value***

Healing from the inside out	100%
Extreme weight loss	100%
Spreading the good news	100%
Consuming all that the Lamb offers	100%
Living in your place at the table	100%
Becoming just like Jesus	100%

*The % Daily Value (DV) tells you how much a nutrient in a serving contributes to a daily diet. Feasting on His Fullness every day is recommended for heavenly nutritional health.

DESSERT

Wedding Cake

For today's dessert I want you to imagine that it is the day of your marriage to Jesus. We are preparing the wedding cake, and it is filled with your wedding vows. I want you to take some time and think about how you would write out your wedding vows to Jesus. The Word is filled with His vows to us. Your wedding vows are promises and commitments to Him that are personal and unique between you and Him. Once you are ready, I want you to write your vows down. Keep them. Re-read them after some time has gone by. Be reminded of how much He means to you.

RESOURCES

Scripture quotations marked AMP are taken from the Amplified® Bible (AMP), Copyright © 2015 by The Lockman Foundation. Used by permission. lockman.org"

Scripture quotations marked AMPC are taken from the Amplified Bible Copyright © 1954, 1958, 1962, 1964, 1965, 1987 by The Lockman Foundation, La Habra, CA. All rights reserved. Used by Permission. www.lockman.org.

Scripture quotations marked CEB are taken from the COMMON ENGLISH BIBLE. © Copyright 2011 COMMON ENGLISH BIBLE. All rights reserved. Used by permission. (www.CommonEnglishBible.com).

Scripture quotations marked CEV are taken from the Contemporary English Version Copyright © 1991, 1992, 1995 by American Bible Society, Used by Permission.

Scripture quotations marked CJB are taken from the Complete Jewish Bible by David H. Stern. Copyright © 1998. All rights reserved. Used by permission of Messianic Jewish Publishers, 6120 Day Long Lane, Clarksville, MD 21029. www.messianicjewish.net.

Scripture quotations marked CSB are taken from The Christian Standard Bible. Copyright © 2017 by Holman Bible Publishers. Used by permission. Christian Standard Bible®, and CSB® are federally registered trademarks of Holman Bible Publishers, all rights reserved.

Scripture quotations marked ESV are taken from the ESV® Bible (The Holy Bible, English Standard Version®). ESV® Text Edition: 2016. Copyright © 2001 by Crossway, a publishing ministry of Good News Publishers. The ESV® text has been reproduced in cooperation with and by permission of Good News Publishers. Unauthorized reproduction of this publication is prohibited. All rights reserved.

Montgomery New Testament (1924) by Helen Barrett Montgomery.

Alexander the Great Quotes. BrainyQuote.com, BrainyMedia Inc, 2024. https://www.brainyquote.com/quotes/alexander_the_great_391181, accessed January 18, 2024.

Psychology Today https://www.psychologytoday.com/us/blog/enlightened-living/200808/core-truths-core-beliefs-and-obstacles-progress-pt-2

Dictionary definitions, not otherwise stated, are found at merriam-webster.com.

Clarke, Adam. (No known publication date). "Romans." In Romans to the Revelations. Vol. 6 of Clarke's Commentary, 93-107. New York: Abingdon-Cokesbury Press.

Cooke, Graham. (2014). Manifesting Your Spirit: Brillant Book House.

Strong, James. Strong's Expanded Exhaustive Concordance of the Bible. Nashville: Thomas Nelson, 2009.

Thayer, Joseph Henry. Greek-English Lexicon of the New Testament. New York: American (Harper), 1889. Blue Letter Bible. 1996-2012.

"G4697 - splagchnizomai - Strong's Greek Lexicon (lxx)." Blue Letter Bible. Accessed 30 Oct, 2023. https://www.blueletterbible.org/lexicon/g4697/lxx/lxx/0-1/

"G907 - baptizō - Strong's Greek Lexicon (lxx)." Blue Letter Bible. Accessed 3 Nov, 2023. https://www.blueletterbible.org/lexicon/g907/lxx/lxx/0-1/

Made in the USA
Columbia, SC
16 July 2024

38448639R10133